3 CRUCIAL QUESTIONS ABOUT THE BIBLE

Grant R. Osborne

Published by Baker Books
a division of Baker Book House Company
P.O. Box 6287, Grand Rapids, MI 49516-6287

Printed in the United States of America

Unless otherwise indicated, Scripture is taken from the HOLY BIBLE, NEW
INTERNATIONAL VERSION®. NIV®. Copyright © 1973, 1978, 1984 by
International Bible Society. Used by permission of Zondervan Publishing House.
All rights reserved. Other versions cited include the Jerusalem Bible (JB), the King
James Version (KJV), the Living Bible (LB), the New American Standard Bible
(NASB), the New English Bible (NEB), the New King James Version (NKJV), the New
Revised Standard Version (NRSV), the Revised Standard Version (RSV), and Today's
English Version (TEV).

The five figures that appear in the text have been reprinted from *The Hermeneutical
Spiral* by Grant R. Osborne. © 1991 by Grant R. Osborne. Used by permission of
InterVarsity Press, P.O. Box 1400, Downers Grove, IL 60515.

ISBN 0-8010-5273-4

Library of Congress Cataloging-in-Publication data on file in Washington, D.C.

To
My parents-in-law
Albert and Mary Hardy
For allowing me to marry
Their wonderful daughter

Contents

Editors' Preface

The books in the 3 Crucial Questions series are the published form of the 3 Crucial Questions Seminars, which are sponsored by Bridge Ministries of Detroit, Michigan. The seminars and books are designed to greatly enhance your Christian walk. The following comments will help you appreciate the unique features of the book series.

The 3 Crucial Questions series is based on two fundamental observations. First, there are crucial questions related to the Christian faith for which imperfect Christians seem to have no final answers. Christians living in eternal glory may know fully even as they are known by God, but now we know only in part (1 Cor. 13:12). Therefore, we must ever return to such questions with the prayer that God the Holy Spirit will continue to lead us nearer to "the truth, the whole truth, and nothing but the truth." While recognizing their own frailty, the authors contributing to this series pray that they are thus led.

Second, each Christian generation partly affirms its solidarity with the Christian past by reaffirming "the faith which was once delivered unto the saints" (Jude 3 KJV). Such an affirmation is usually attempted by religious scholars who are notorious for talking only to themselves or by nonexperts whose grasp of the faith lacks depth of insight. Both situations are unfortunate, but we feel that our team of contributing authors is well

7

prepared to avoid them. Each author is a competent Christian scholar able to share tremendous learning in down-to-earth language both laity and experts can appreciate. In a word, you have in hand a book that is part of a rare series, one that is neither pedantic nor pediatric.

The topics addressed in the series have been chosen for their timelessness, interest level, and importance to Christians everywhere. And the contributing authors are committed to discussing them in a manner that promotes Christian unity. They discuss not only areas of disagreement among Christians but significant areas of agreement as well. Seeking peace and pursuing it as the Bible commands (1 Peter 3:11), they stress common ground on which Christians with different views may meet for wholesome dialogue and reconciliation.

The books in the series consist not merely of printed words; they consist of words to live by. Their pages are filled not only with good information but with sound instruction in successful Christian living. For study is truly Christian only when, in addition to helping us understand our faith, it helps us to live our faith. We pray therefore that you will allow God to use the 3 Crucial Questions series to augment your growth in the grace and knowledge of our Lord and Savior Jesus Christ.

Grant R. Osborne
Richard J. Jones, Jr.

Author's Preface

I am producing this book for lay people rather than professionals, for I am convinced that the Bible is intended primarily for them and not just for the academy. There is unprecedented interest in God's Word; consider, for example, not only the production of new translations and study Bibles for virtually every interest group, but also the number of people attending Bible studies. This is an exciting time with enormous potential. Yet questions abound, and people need both an assurance that the Bible is reliable and a method enabling them to study the Bible for themselves.

Very little has been written on why we can trust the Bible as the Word of God. My greatest shock in doing chapter 1 was the paucity of material produced over the last couple of decades on the subject of biblical reliability. Yet there is more and more bombardment from the left wing against the accuracy and trustworthiness of Scripture; tragically, the attacks of the Jesus Seminar, a media favorite, have prompted too few evangelical responses that the average Christian can understand. It is my hope that this volume will help in this area. I have found that Christians do wonder how to defend the Bible from attacks and do care that in many churches it is treated as just another source for material on how to live religiously. Many have friends and relatives who assume the Bible is filled with errors and is merely a product of the religious experiences of people in the past. Others know an individual who has been drawn into a cult but don't know how to point out the biblical errors in its teachings. Few have witnessed to people for very long without being asked why the Bible should be placed above other books. Reliability is an essential issue.

At the same time few actually know how to study the Bible. The subject of hermeneutics (principles for interpreting Scripture) has become a fad, but there is too little "trickle-down" to the people in the pew on how to study Scripture for devotions or for teaching a Bible class. Often after I have delivered a message, someone will ask, "Where did you find that?" I am always excited when I encounter that question, because I know I have found a person seriously interested in deep Bible study. I believe there are a great many persons like that, and this book is written for them. My belief is that anyone who cares can begin to study and understand Scripture at a deep level. It does take dedication and time, but so does everything worthwhile in life. Imagine what would happen if Christians all over the world started spending as much time and money on studying the Word as they do golfing or skiing or working out. Why not "scriptural aerobics"?

While little has been written on reliability and on hermeneutics, virtually nothing has been produced on how to formulate theology. This is true even at the academic level, let alone at the lay level. The process of reformulating a church's doctrinal statement or working through a major theological controversy in the church has virtually been left to whimsy. Very few know how to do it correctly, and that is why so many cults have had their origins in evangelical churches; yet at the other extreme people have been accused of heresy for every little issue. This book attempts to provide a way of deciding which of the many doctrinal claims are actually supported by Scripture, which constitute heresy, and which should be labeled theological differences rather than false teaching.

Can We Trust the Bible?

Trust is an essential ingredient in any relationship. "To trust" means to accept something for what it claims to be, to believe in it, to act in faith that it will do its part. A quarterback needs to trust both his linemen and his receivers in order to complete a pass. Salespeople must trust their product before they can convince others to buy it. And we must trust the Bible before we can accept it as the Word of God and base our lives upon its teaching. There are many levels to trusting the Bible. When we say that we trust the Bible, we may mean that we consider it to be good literature, a set of fine principles to ponder, or divine revelation that must be obeyed.

About three out of every four invitations that I receive to various campuses to speak to student groups involve requests to lecture on the authority of Scripture. University religion profs bombard students with the supposed unreliability of Scripture, with all the problems in maintaining a high view of its authority, and with the prevalent conception that it is a human book, certainly one of the greatest human achievements in history, but nevertheless the product of human religious experience rather than divine revelation. This judgment is normally based on the so-called errors in the Bible and the consensus of "higher" scholarship. My task in speaking on campuses and in writing this book is to counter these arguments and to present a case for the Bible as divine and human, both revealed by God and written by human authors (under divine inspiration). This has been the view of the church for two thousand years, and it is still the best option for today.

In this chapter we will begin by surveying different views of biblical authority, moving from the evangelical to the various nonevangelical approaches. We will not be surveying church history, because until the post-Enlightenment period there was significant agreement that the Bible is the Word of God.[1] Instead, we will consider the views of this century, especially those that are still influential. In the next section we will present a case for a high view of the Bible's authority as the inerrant or infallible Word of God. There we will proceed from the Bible's own statements about itself to an apologetic for the Christian faith (specifically for the resurrection and hence the divinity of Jesus) and through that for the authority of Scripture. We will take this approach because people's views of Scripture are intimately bound up with their views of God and his presence in this world. There can be no faith in the Bible without faith in God and Christ, and arguments for the Bible proceed necessarily from arguments for the Christian faith as a whole. Finally, we will study several key problem passages (which detractors usually call errors) to show the viability of the evangelical position. My view is that the doctrine of inerrancy is both deductive (proceeding from a logical assessment of divine revelation) and inductive (proceeding from the study of the Bible itself). Our investigation of this doctrine will be both deductive and inductive because all the logic in the world is valueless if there are actual errors in the Bible.

Views of Biblical Authority

1. The Evangelical View

The evangelical position on biblical authority is in keeping with the dogma of the church for its first seventeen centuries. This teaching was one of the few doctrines that the Reformers and the Catholic church held in common. The focal point of this position is the doctrine of divine revelation. The very meaning of "revelation" centers on God's making known his existence, presence, and involvement with humankind. There are two types— general revelation, as God makes himself known through nature (Ps. 19:1–2; Rom. 1:19–20), and special revelation, as God reveals himself, his plan, and his relationship to humans through the Bible. Nature, of course, cannot do more than make one aware of the existence of God and the finiteness of humans. The details must be filled in by Scripture. Moreover, revelation in Scripture entails propositional truth. Some have tried to argue that it is not knowledge of God but a personal relation with God that is the actual result of revelation. If this is true, the Bible does not produce doctrine but faith-encounter. Yet this is too disjunctive; what the Bible actually produces is a both-and rather than an either-or. It imparts information and through that information calls the reader to commitment.

God has revealed himself and his will via inspiration, the process by which the Spirit guided the sacred writers of Scripture to record God's revealed truths. As Paul said in his classic statement in 2 Timothy 3:16, "All Scripture is God-breathed." However, this does not give rise to a dictation theory that God told the writers exactly what to say, for it is clear that each author wrote in his own style and wording. For instance, some New Testament books exhibit excellent Greek (Luke-Acts, Hebrews, James, 1 Peter) while others exhibit average or even poor Greek (John, Revelation, 2 Peter). By "inspiration," then, we mean that God guided the authors as they wrote in their own words.

Of course, when the prophets told Israel, "Thus says the LORD," there was a kind of dictation, but that related to specific messages from God written down in the prophetic book rather than actual dictation of the whole book. Therefore, we would hold to verbal inspiration rather than dictation—that is, God inspired all the words of Scripture but did not mechanically dictate them.

Finally, most evangelicals hold to the inerrancy or infallibility of Scripture: it is completely truthful and without error in the original autographs.[2] The purpose of this doctrine is to safeguard the absolute authority of God's Word. However, the definition and even relevance of the term *inerrant* have been the subject of heated debate within evangelicalism. Many want to replace "inerrant" with "infallible" because of the exclusivity of the term. Others propound a "limited inerrancy," saying that the Bible is without error in matters of salvation and dogma but not in matters of science or history.[3] Most evangelicals, however, take a view of full inerrancy that sees the Bible as without error in all it intends to say. They point out that the Bible does not always intend to relate exact scientific or historical information but describes some events phenomenologically, that is, as people then saw them. When we say "the sun rises" or "the sun sets," we do not mean it literally. The same is true of many statements in Scripture. For instance, when Jesus called the mustard seed "the smallest seed you plant in the ground" (Mark 4:31), he was not making a scientific statement but was using rabbinic hyperbole; his point was that no other seed that small produces such a large plant. To sum up the evangelical view of the authority of Scripture, we might simply list the three terms we have been elaborating—revelation, inspiration, inerrancy.

2. The Neoorthodox View

In 1919 Karl Barth, a young pastor writing in the academic vacuum caused by World War I (which destroyed the optimistic humanism of the German intelligentsia), published his Romans commentary. It caused a sensation and produced a "new ortho-doxy" that largely controlled theological thinking on the Con-tinent for more than a generation. Barth argued that we cannot encounter God; rather, God encounters us through "flashes of insight" as we read the Bible. Barth was trying to find a middle ground between the rigid orthodoxy of the fundamentalist camp and the dead liberalism of his training. He found it by conceiv-ing of the Bible not as the Word of God, but as the instrument of the "Word of God," which he defined as the "dialectic" (hence the term *dialectical theology*) that God establishes whenever he decides to speak to us through the Bible. Thus the Bible is the means of God's Word to us rather than the Word itself.[4]

Barth accepted the Calvinist teaching of the utter sinfulness of humanity and the absolute sovereignty of God. He believed that people on their own cannot find God. J. I. Packer nicely summa-rizes Barth's position as "a substantially Nicene Trinitarianism, a Chalcedonian Christology, an acknowledgment of Jesus' death and resurrection as the work of God saving mankind, and a robust con-fidence that the biblical witness to Jesus Christ, which is God's own witness given through man's, can be truly and precisely expressed in the propositions and theses of rational, disciplined theological discourse."[5] Throughout his life and voluminous writings, Barth became more and more conservative, though his instrumental view of Scripture never truly changed. Nor did he ever repudiate his belief that the Bible contains factual errors (though, ironically, he never really discussed any) and is at heart a human book (though he always interpreted it as if it were fully authoritative!). So in Barth's view the Bible is the means by which revelation occurs rather than the product of revelation. Inspiration is more God's work with the present reader than God's work with the past author, though it does encompass both (since God was equally at work in the reli-gious experience of the original author).[6]

Obviously, there is an inconsistency between Barth's theory and his practice; in addition, the subjectivity that results from his emphasis on divine encounter over propositional communication is a fatal flaw. Roger Nicole finds eight weaknesses in Barth's approach:

1. Barth has replaced the doctrine of the authority of Scripture with the concept that God is free to speak through Scripture.
2. Barth ignores the Bible's claims to be revelation (and not just a witness to revelation).
3. The view that the Bible is fallible but becomes the Word of God is inconsistent.
4. Barth's claim to have recaptured the Reformation view does not square with Martin Luther's and John Calvin's clear statements that the Bible is (not that it becomes) the Word of God.
5. Barth is weak on the canon of Scripture; while affirming the canon as we have it, he allows for the possibility of further canonical works.
6. Without making an examination he declares that there are errors and contradictions in Scripture.
7. Without providing any reasons he asserts that the Bible is the only channel through which God speaks (Emil Brunner on the other hand believes there are many channels).
8. Barth's view of divine transcendence and sovereignty leads him to reject natural revelation and could lead to a distortion of Christology.[7]

3. The Existential View

Existentialism rejects Western metaphysics and the Christian heritage of the Bible as the Word of God, and replaces them with the human being's struggle with the problems of existence (anxiety, guilt, death). People rather than external forces are in charge of their own fate and must transcend their struggle with finitude. As followers of Martin Heidegger's philosophy, Rudolf

Bultmann and Paul Tillich identified biblical truth with existential concerns.

In the early 1920s Bultmann had been a follower of Barth and become neoorthodoxy's left-wing New Testament critic. However, from 1923 to 1928 he taught with Heidegger at the University of Marburg and reworked his theology. Basically he believed that science has made it impossible to accept a supernatural base for the Bible, and that one has to "demythologize" or remove all "mythical" (which he identified as anything supernatural) elements from the Bible to make it meaningful.[8] The primary tool for arriving at the relevance of the biblical message is existentialism. The mythical is not so much to be thrown out as reinterpreted to reflect the true scriptural message regarding the human struggle with existence. This message centers upon the struggle between a life of the flesh (inauthentic existence) and a life of faith (authentic existence). The way to move from inauthentic to authentic existence is through decision making, through living for the future rather than living in the past. For Bultmann the resurrection was not a historical event but a reflection of the church's faith in the possibilities of the future.

Paul Tillich was primarily a philosophical theologian who also applied existentialism to religious truth. He saw God not as a personal being, but as the Ground of Being or Being itself. God does not exist in a finite sense, but is the principle of life or being through which everything exists. As such he is not so much outside things as within them. In this sense people experience God when they experience life. It is in the struggles of existence that God is found; this is not a personal relationship but an interaction with life. For Tillich the Bible is only one of many sources in which God can be experienced. It is the basic source of Christian theology because it records the origins of the Christian movement, those events through which humans existentially encountered and witnessed to Jesus as the New Being, the first to become "transparent" to the Ground of Being.

Yet the Bible is not the norm or final arbiter of truth; rather, it attests to the truth of "ultimate concern" as that truth is found in Jesus as the New Being. Revelation occurs when individuals experience the mystery of life, of ultimate concern in the Ground of Being. The Bible is in no sense revelatory but can guide one to revelatory experiences.[9]

It is obvious that existentialist approaches differ radically from the classic view of revelation and inspiration. When revelation becomes an existential openness to reality, and inspiration becomes a present experience of overcoming finitude, the Bible's own understanding of divine transcendence and propositional truth has been rejected. The call to decision in the present is not a salvific event but a grappling with existence. The Bible is not the Word of God but a set of symbols or myths to be re-interpreted on the basis of the immense problems of daily existence. This view is diametrically opposed to essential evangelical beliefs—a personal God who has revealed himself propositionally in the Bible, which is the Word of God. For us the solution to the problems of existence is salvation in Christ.[10]

4. Liberationist and Feminist Views

What is called the sociocritical school argues that the Bible has been used to oppress minority groups (the poor, women, blacks) and that the authoritarian aspects must be removed before it can speak authoritatively. This school also believes that the relevance of the Bible is not in its propositional content (its past dimension) but in its ability to liberate oppressed minorities (its present dimension). Among the leading theorists are Jürgen Habermas and Karl-Otto Apel, who declare that interpretation must begin with a critique of ideology, namely a realization that words are controlled by social forces that manipulate texts and are manipulated by texts. The written word then exerts a subtle but distinct influence over every reader and is often used to control people's thinking. Habermas wants to make this ideological pressure obvious and to help the reader to be aware of it. His goal is to unmask the social world behind both text and interpreter, thus liberating both.[11]

Liberation, black, and feminist theologies extend this socio-critical goal to social action. The interpreter does not merely critique but changes both texts and societies that oppress. Since Western society manipulates the theology of heaven to tell the poor that their reward is in the next life, the task of the true Christian is to liberate the poor from such manipulations and the oppressive systems that have developed from them. Liberation theologians redefine sin as socioeconomic oppression, salvation as liberation, faith as praxis, and knowledge as the transformation of society. For feminist theologians the Bible must be liberated from male-dominated interpretation, including the patriarchal views in the Bible itself. Rosemary Radford Ruether believes that the key is to see women's experience as a "critical force, exposing classical theology, including its foundational tradition in scripture, as shaped by male experience rather than human experience."[12]

Certainly there is some truth in the sociocritical school. Social forces have misused the Bible, and ideology does all too often control interpretation. The plight of the poor, of minorities like blacks and women, has been justified by a great deal of theological manipulation. However, the critical assumptions and biblical perspective of the liberationist theologies are highly flawed. Scripture is frequently viewed as human experience rather than the Word of God, and some of its teachings (e.g., social justice) are elevated above others (e.g., spiritual salvation). The redefinition of key doctrines is a perversion of biblical truth. Most of all, these theologies break their own rules, critiquing the social forces behind the Bible and society but failing to critique themselves. In short, while the Bible mandates that the Christian seek social justice and alleviate the suffering of the oppressed, an approach which diminishes the Bible's status as the Word of God and places it under the control of social needs is inadequate.

5. Recent Roman Catholic Views

Until the last fifty years or so the Roman Catholic Church had a view of biblical authority even more conservative than the evangelical view. In 1546 the Council of Trent said the Bible was "dictated either orally by Christ or by the Holy Ghost," and in 1870 the First Vatican Council said the Scriptures "contain revelation, with no admixture of error . . . having been written by the inspiration of the Holy Ghost, they have God for their author" (*Constitution on Revelation* 2). In 1893 Pope Leo XIII's encyclical *Providentissimus Deus* (23) said:

> All the books which the Church receives as sacred and canonical, are written wholly and entirely, with all their parts, at the dictation of the Holy Ghost; and so far is it from possible that any error can co-exist with inspiration, that inspiration not only is essentially incompatible with error, but excludes and rejects it as absolutely and necessarily as it is impossible that God himself, the Supreme Truth, can utter that which is not true.[13]

Traditionally Catholics have also held a virtual dictation view of inspiration and a corresponding distrust of modern critical methods as espoused by Protestant scholars. The major debate until recently did not concern revelation and inspiration, but the extent of biblical authority and its relationship to the authority of tradition.

The change began in 1941 when the Biblical Commission of Pope Pius XII "condemned an overly conservative distrust of modern biblical research"; in 1943 the papal encyclical *Divino Afflante Spiritu* actually encouraged critical methods. From that time increasing numbers of young scholars were trained in higher criticism. A conservative reaction occurred, and skeptical conclusions were largely rejected by the Holy Office. At Vatican II (1962–65), however, compromise ruled the day, and the final result was an ambiguous statement recognizing the validity of the historical-critical approach and in effect nullifying the historical inerrantist position of Roman Catholicism.

Hans Küng, professor at the University of Tübingen and one of the most powerful spokesmen of the New Catholicism (even though his status as an official Catholic theologian was revoked in 1979), argues that theological discussion should begin with human experience (from below) rather than with the Bible (from above). In his famous work *Infallible?* (1972) he denies the final authority not only of the pope but of Scripture as well. In his best-seller *On Being a Christian* (1971) he "called many NT stories uncertain, contradictory, and legendary, rejected Chalcedonian Christology, weakened God's transcendence in favor of humanization, and seemed to present Christ more as an example to follow than a divine Savior in whom to trust."[14] Jesus, not the Bible, is the final revelation of God to humankind; this revelation is mediated by Scripture, but Scripture is a fallible witness because it no longer speaks directly but must be interpreted anew by each generation. The biblical books are the product of the religious experience of human authors, and this fallible witness becomes truth only when used by the Spirit of truth.

Karl Rahner, another great Roman Catholic theologian of the late-twentieth century, takes a consciously existential (he studied under Heidegger) and human-centered approach to religious reality. For Rahner as for Küng, there is little room for a divine intervention from outside this cosmos. So divine revelation is not external but internal, a self-communication from within our experience of the world and God's transcendental place in it. It is not objective but subjective. It reached final form in Jesus, but it is experienced anew in the church. The authority of Scripture is not in proposition but in its witness to Jesus and the launching of the church, through which the inspiring power of the Spirit is seen. Obviously, in Küng and Rahner Catholicism's traditionally high view of Scripture has been replaced by a view akin to that of Barth and even Bultmann.

6. Postmodern Perspectives

More and more, critics in the last decade have labeled themselves "postmodern," which can be defined as a critical rejection of both the authority of the text and the historical-critical method, which distances the text from the reader. Purportedly, postmodernism "challenges an intellectual certitude that is the antithesis of freedom, faith, and imagination, but it does not support a lapse into irrationality."[15] The movement is characterized by a rejection of all authority and a corresponding radical pluralism that welcomes all fresh ideas.

In literary analysis the postmodern rejection of all final authority (especially religious authority) is built upon the radical autonomy of the text (that is to say, once it is written, the text is free or autonomous from the author's intended meaning), the centrality of the reader in interpretation, and a radical pluralism or openness toward other interpretations or beliefs. In the postmodern arena, there is no specific meaning, but only possible meanings. Therefore any idea of a divinely inspired revelation is discarded by definition.

Two primary proponents should be discussed. Jacques Derrida is a highly influential philosopher who spearheads the movement called "deconstruction," which states that every text is open to any number of possible understandings and so must be "deconstructed" or removed from the author's (and everyone else's) interpretation. In other words, the text is a playground on which a reader can play any number of games, all of them equally valid. Derrida, a follower of Friedrich Nietzsche, argues for a rhetorical approach to meaning that says there are no controls, only freedom to construct one's own understanding.[16] The Bible obviously ceases to be a divinely inspired book, and becomes primarily an opportunity for the reader to play, so to speak, and to search for new religious paradigms (though Derrida himself is an avowed atheist).

Stanley Fish is the major proponent of reader-response criticism, an American literary movement that says meaning is constructed by the reader rather than by the text. For Fish meaning results from a reading strategy provided by the reading community to which one belongs. This means that one's understanding of the Bible depends upon whether one belongs to a Baptist, a Lutheran, or a Reformed community. There is no actual meaning in the Bible; it is an open field and awaits a reader to create meaning through the act of reading. For Fish, neither text nor reader has autonomy; both fuse or unite at the moment of reading and are re-created into a new entity.[17] When such a position is applied to the Bible, it is clear there can be no concept of revelation or objective authority. All the authority is with the reader and the community. Inspiration refers to a cleverly devised interpretation.

A Case for the Reliability of Scripture

As evangelicals we believe that the Bible is the Word of God, without error in its original autographs, and the product of divine revelation. Chosen individuals in Israel and the early church were inspired to put this revelation into their own words and were guided by the Holy Spirit to give us the message God wished. As John MacArthur has said:

> God inspired every word of the original manuscripts, and they are without error in every detail. The Bible is the only completely trustworthy source of knowledge about God. Man can't learn all he needs to know about God from human reason, philosophy, or even experience. God alone is the source of the knowledge about Himself, and He has chosen to reveal Himself in the Bible and in no other book.[18]

We believe this, but how can we know it for sure? What evidence can we adduce for a high view of Scripture? Is it really the only completely trustworthy source of divine revelation, and is it the final and absolute arbiter of faith and conduct for the believer? In this section we will approach this topic by a logical series of five steps. First, we need to see what the Bible has to say for itself. Second, we will consider whether the resurrection of Jesus can be proven or disproven, and then proceed to the implications for his teaching about the Bible. Third, we will note that the process that established the Old and New Testament canon was God-controlled and hence reliable. Fourth, we will see that text criticism helps us to ascertain the actual words of the authors. Fifth, we will consider a few miscellaneous arguments for the reliability of Scripture.

1. The Witness of Scripture to Itself

It is one of the basic laws of jurisprudence that every witness is respected and given credence unless disproven or discredited. From Roman times to the present, every person has been allowed to present one's own case in court. Therefore, even the greatest skeptic is required by the laws of fairness to listen to the Bible's own claims for itself. This of course will not prove that they are correct, but it will tell us what we are examining, that is, how the biblical writers viewed what they wrote. Did the writer of the Book of Jonah consider it to be fiction or history? Were the prophets giving their own educated guesses or relating God's message for Israel? Did the Evangelists believe they were writing what actually had occurred, that is, eyewitness accounts, and not simply stories they had heard?

Throughout the Old Testament, God is seen speaking directly to people. The Ten Commandments begins with, "And God spoke all these words," and afterwards the people beg Moses, "Do not have God speak to us or we will die" (Exod. 20:1, 19). It is clear that the biblical account has God speaking audibly and directly. Similar examples can be found throughout the Old Testament (e.g., Gen. 1, 3, 12, 15, 17, 18), which could be said to center upon the direct communication between God and his chosen people. In fact, Israel's episodes of apostasy were precisely those times when they failed to heed God's voice.

Speeches by the prophets were also viewed as God's words. Here, for example, we frequently find the phrase "Thus says Yahweh," which reflects a royal-decree formula often used in the ancient Near East to introduce the words of a king to his vassals (see, e.g., Isa. 36–37). Everything said by the prophet in God's name had its source in God, a fact often stated directly ("the LORD made this prophecy" and "declares the LORD" in 2 Kings 9:25–26) and even in the first person ("I am the LORD" in Isa. 45:5). Moreover, it is often said that God spoke "through" the prophet, an indication that the saying originated with God, not the prophet (1 Kings 14:18; 16:12). One's response to the prophet's message was one's response to God; to disobey the prophet was to disobey the voice of the Lord (1 Kings 20:35–36). Also regarded as divine sayings were the written words in the canon ("Moses wrote all the words of the LORD" [Exod. 24:4 RSV] and "Joshua wrote these words in the book of the law of God" [Josh. 24:26 RSV]). Thus three different forms of Old Testament sayings are attributed to God: direct speech to the people, messages given through prophets, and written records inscribed by chosen individuals.[19]

Gleason Archer notes the awareness on the part of Old Testament authors that they were narrating actual historical events: "The Old Testament shows no awareness whatever of any supposed line of distinction between theological doctrine and miraculous events."[20] This means that the authors believed they were describing actual historical events rather than telling stories with a theological message. In both the Old and New Testaments we cannot separate the historical from the theological. There are both history and theology in the biblical narratives. For some

examples of the Old Testament's awareness of its factuality,
Archer points to Psalm 105, which reaffirms the history of the
ten plagues on Egypt (Exod. 7–12), and to Psalm 106, which
celebrates the historical event of the parting of the Red Sea. Isaiah 28:21 and 1 Kings 16:34 affirm, respectively, the factuality
of the battle of Gibeon and the fall of the walls of Jericho.

In similar fashion Wayne Grudem discusses passages that
reflect the Old Testament's understanding regarding its charac-
ter and authority.[21] In Numbers 23:19 Balaam says, "God is not
a man, that he should lie" (see also 1 Sam. 15:29), meaning that
God is incapable of telling a falsehood; his sayings are completely
reliable. Deuteronomy 4:2 and 12:32 forbid adding to and taking from God's commands. They are unique and complete in
authority, beyond human improvement. Psalm 12:6 says, "The
words of the LORD are pure" (KJV), like silver refined seven times
in the furnace. The picture is of absolute perfection ("purified
seven times"), a total absence of imperfection. Could the author
of these words ever have accepted the possibility of factual errors
in the biblical text? Another group of passages (Ps. 18:30;
119:140; Prov. 30:5) speaks of the Word of the Lord as "flaw-
less" or "thoroughly tested," a term that means "without imperfection, completely reliable." Psalm 119:89 speaks of the Word
as "firmly fixed in the heavens" (RSV), meaning it is eternally fixed
and cannot be altered, and verse 96 calls it "exceedingly broad"
or limitless in its effects. Psalm 119:160 says, "The sum of your
word is truth, and every one of your righteous ordinances endures
forever" (NRSV), meaning that it is eternal truth that can never
be changed. Like God, his revealed Word is immutable (unchanging from generation to generation). Proverbs 8:8 states the same
truth negatively, "All the words of my mouth are righteous; there
is nothing twisted or crooked in them" (RSV). There is never a
need to straighten a crooked path or correct a false statement in
God's revealed Word; it is at all times reliable. On the basis of
these passages, we have to say that the Old Testament shows as

much awareness of the complete trustworthiness of Scripture as do the better-known New Testament passages.

The New Testament also treats the Old Testament as the Word of God. For instance, the formulae that call Old Testament passages to mind often point to God or the Holy Spirit as the author, as in Acts 1:16 ("The Holy Spirit spoke beforehand," RSV) and Hebrews 1:5–13 ("God says . . . he says"). Throughout the New Testament the teachings of the Old Testament are seen as the final authority for all truth. Whenever Paul, Peter, or one of the other New Testament writers wants to present a foolproof argument, he appeals to the Old Testament. Every Old Testament allusion in Hebrews, 1 Peter, and Revelation, which are notable for their number of quotations, shows and demands absolute allegiance to and agreement with the Old Testament. As Jesus said, every "iota" and "dot" (the smallest units in Hebrew writing) has authority (Matt. 5:18 RSV). Moreover, the New Testament regards the smallest Old Testament historical details as authentic. Grudem gives a partial list: David's eating the consecrated bread in the temple (Matt. 12:3–4); Jonah in the whale (Matt. 12:40); Nineveh's repenting (Matt. 12:41); the Queen of the South's visit to Solomon (Matt. 12:42); the murder of Zechariah (Matt. 23:35); Elijah's being sent to the widow of Zarephath (Luke 4:25–26); Naaman's being cleansed of leprosy (Luke 4:27); the destruction of Sodom by fire and brimstone (Luke 17:29); Lot's wife turned to salt (Luke 17:32); Moses' lifting up the serpent in the wilderness (John 3:14).[22] The list could go on and on (Grudem has seventeen more), but the point has been made. As far as the New Testament is concerned, the Old Testament is fully authoritative and historically verifiable. Of course, the New Testament citations do not state categorically that the Old Testament events are historically trustworthy, but do treat them implicitly as such; and, as we will argue throughout this chapter, the burden of proof is on the skeptic to prove they are *not* historical, not on us to prove they are. Taken as a whole, the New Testament texts are quite clear: the Old Testament records actual events, not fictional stories.

Finally, let us consider the New Testament witness to itself. Here the statements are not as strong as the statements in the Old Testament writings. Nevertheless, there are several indicators of a self-conscious sense of inspiration. Let us begin with what I would call the three steps to the canon, that is, three preliminary stages that led the early church to consciousness of the canon.

The first stage is the special respect accorded to the sayings of Jesus, which from the start the church regarded as equal to the Old Testament in authority. The Epistles do not contain a lot of quotations of Jesus' sayings, but those we do find are significant for our purposes.[23] Let us begin with 1 Thessalonians, which is either the first or second epistle Paul wrote (this depends on when one dates Galatians). Many believe that 2:14–16 contains allusions to Matthew 23:29–38; especially in view are the references to killing the prophets, heaping up sins to the limit, and the coming of God's wrath. More explicit is 4:13–5:11, which deals with the return of Christ. In 4:15 Paul says this is "according to the Lord's own word," and the whole passage reflects the Olivet Discourse (Mark 13 and parallels). In Romans there are no direct quotes but several allusions to the teachings of Jesus (e.g., 12:14, 17; 13:7, 8–9; 14:10, 14; 16:19). In these Paul, to establish his points, is consciously building on Jesus' teaching. In 1 Corinthians Paul quotes Jesus three times. In 7:10, the saying against divorce, Paul declares, "Not I, but the Lord [says]." In 7:12 he reverses this: "I say this (I, not the Lord)." It is likely that "the Lord [says]" refers to a quote, and "I say" to Paul's own command (note that in 7:40 his statement is said to be from the Spirit of God, so it does not have a lesser authority). In 9:14 Paul's contention that a pastor should be paid is buttressed by a clear allusion to Luke 10:7: "the Lord has commanded that those who preach the gospel should receive their living from the gospel." Finally, in 1 Corinthians 11:23–25 Paul begins the words of institution with an allusion to Luke 22:19–20: "For I received from the Lord what I also passed on to you." These examples contradict the belief of several New Testament critics that Paul knew very little about the Jesus tradition or ignored the Logia Jesu (sayings of Jesus). Clearly he utilized Jesus' teachings frequently and gave them a status equal to that of the Old Testament. This is especially exemplified in the Pauline statement in 1 Timothy 5:18 on the necessity of paying ministers of the gospel, where Luke 10:7 is quoted alongside Deuteronomy 25:4, and both are introduced by the formula, "For the Scripture says." It is clear that Paul placed the sayings of Jesus alongside the Old Testament as canon.

The second stage of a growing canon-consciousness is the particular attention that the Epistles devoted to creeds and hymns. It is noteworthy that the two writers who most frequently anchored their teaching in the creeds are Paul and Peter, the two major apostles. The creeds were developed by the apostles both to enhance worship and to protect from false teaching. Succinct and memorable summaries of key doctrines, they were used in the Epistles to prove or anchor particular arguments. Among the credal material in the Pauline Epistles are doxologies, hymns, liturgical expressions, and confessional utterances like "Abba, Father," "Maranatha," and "Amen." The primary focus of most of the creeds and hymns is the person and work of Christ, especially his incarnation (Phil. 2:6–8), humiliation and exaltation (Phil. 2:6–11; Rom. 4:24 and 8:32), saving work (Rom. 10:8–10; 1 Cor. 15:3–5), resurrection (1 Cor. 15:3–8), and exaltation (Col. 1:15–20; 1 Tim. 3:16; Heb. 1:2–3). Among the signs by which credal material can be detected are certain introductory words like "who" and the conjunction "that," verbs like "received" and "passed on," parallel participial or clausal constructions, a strophic pattern in the phrasing, and high christological content, often using terms not common to the author.[24]

The high incidence of credal material in key places in Paul's and Peter's writings (for Peter see, e.g., 1 Peter 1:18–19, 23; 2:21–24; 3:18, 22) gives evidence to the central place it had in the life and worship of the early church. Given that the two greatest apostles in the early church anchor their arguments in the creeds and not simply in their apostolic authority, it seems obvious that the creeds had great status in the church and were another stage toward canon-consciousness.

The third stage is the collection of Paul's epistles. We know from 2 Peter 3:15–16 that Peter was aware of the Pauline letters:

> Bear in mind that our Lord's patience means salvation, just as our dear brother Paul also wrote you with the wisdom that God gave him. He writes the same way in all his letters, speaking in them of these matters. His letters contain some things that are hard to understand, which ignorant and unstable people distort, as they do the other Scriptures, to their own destruction.

Two elements here are particularly important. "All his letters" means that Peter was aware of a corpus, and many scholars believe this indicates that Paul's epistles were already being collected; this would be the first scriptural hint of the development of a New Testament canon. Also, Peter uses the phrase "the other Scriptures," which might well mean that Paul's epistles had already been given canonical status. As Grudem says, "Since *graphē* in the New Testament always refers to the Old Testament Scriptures, which both Jews and Christians held to be the authoritative words of God . . . this is an indication that very early in the history of the church Paul's epistles were considered to be God's written words in the same sense as the Old Testament texts."[25]

Two final passages must be considered as summing up the evidence. The primary text in any discussion of inspiration is 2 Timothy 3:16–17, "All Scripture is God-breathed and is useful for teaching, rebuking, correcting and training in righteousness, so that the man of God may be thoroughly equipped for every good work." While all scholars agree that "Scripture" here refers to the Old Testament (since the other New Testament uses of the term tend to refer to the Old Testament), we can, given the placement of Paul's writings in that category by 2 Peter 3:16, validly place the New Testament under that umbrella as well. Moreover, it is "every Scripture" that is inspired; the Greek *pasa graphē* indicates that every single part of Scripture is God-breathed. This has led to the term "plenary verbal inspiration" to describe the inspiration of every single word of the Bible. Finally, note in 2 Timothy that the purpose of inspiration is not just propositional truth (theology) but changed lives (ethics). The God-breathed Scripture profits believers by teaching, rebuking, correcting, and training them so they might produce good works. Theology is incomplete (even more, it is falsified) if it is not lived in daily conduct.

The second major passage is 2 Peter 1:20–21, "Above all, you must understand that no prophecy of Scripture came about by the prophet's own interpretation. For prophecy never had its origin in the will of man, but men spoke from God as they were carried along by the Holy Spirit." Peter is saying that the Old Testament prophets never spoke on their own volition but prophesied only as they were moved by the Holy Spirit. The image pictured in the verb *pheronomoi* ("were carried along") is that the prophets' thinking was brought forth by the Spirit. The same verb is used earlier in the verse, where it is translated "had its origin in." The two uses of the verb point out that the source of the inspired Word is not the human author but God. This does not mandate a dictation theory maintaining that God told the prophets what to say. For Peter says in the same verse that they "spoke" or wrote their words. He is simply saying that the ultimate source ("origin") is not human thinking but divine inspiration.

2. The Historicity of the Resurrection of Jesus

To sum up our case thus far: the witness of both the Old and New Testament is that God is behind every word, and therefore the whole Bible is both divinely inspired and supremely authoritative. Yet this witness does not prove our case. Thus far we could be guilty of circular reasoning, that is, examining the evidence for an allegedly inspired book from the standpoint of our prior belief that it is an inspired book. That approach proves nothing. What we have shown is that the Bible *claims* to be a book inspired by God. It is up to us now to look at evidence that can prove or disprove that claim.

To evaluate the Bible's claim that it is the Word of God, let us first examine its claim that Jesus rose from the dead.[26] Note that at this stage we cannot assume anything. We cannot assume that the resurrection really happened. Nor can we assume that the Bible is the Word of God, for that is the very thesis we are examining in this chapter. What we must do at this stage is to pretend we are historians and ask whether the claims can be verified.

We begin our assignment as historians by noting that the Bible says a person named Jesus, whom his followers called the Christ, was raised from the dead. Did it really happen? There are techniques for deciding whether Julius Caesar was really assassinated, whether Alexander the Great really defeated the Persians, and whether the god Zeus ever lived. As in other historical studies, we must test the written witnesses for their truthfulness. There are principles for deciding whether a piece of writing is history or fiction. Clarence Walhout says that the difference is the realistic nature of historical material; that is, "the historian claims—asserts—that the projected world (the story) of the text together with the authorial point of view counts as a story and an interpretation of things as they are." Walhout develops four criteria for deciding that the material is historical: (1) the world in the text is factually accurate; (2) the point of view taken by the author has a historical perspective; (3) the circumstances of the text's production and the way it was used by its original readers indicate that it was seen as history rather than fiction; (4) the author's claims regarding the situation or world depicted in the story point to a real rather than fictive world behind the text.[27]

The New Testament claim is quite clear. All four Gospels talk of the resurrection as an event that occurred in space and time. The message of the angel could not be more distinct: "You are looking for Jesus the Nazarene, who was crucified. He has risen! He is not here. See the place where they laid him" (Mark 16:6). That is an empirical statement; the angel points to the burial place and asserts, "He isn't here; he's risen." Matthew comes closest to describing the actual event: "There was a violent earthquake, for an angel of the Lord came down from heaven and . . . rolled back the stone" (28:2). Luke and John emphasize the empirical proof, with Jesus showing the disciples his hands and side and even allowing them to touch his wounds (Luke 24:37–40; John 20:20, 27). In John's account, Peter goes into the tomb and sees both the burial linen and the facecloth "folded up by itself, separate from the linen" (20:6–7). Such details almost certainly have an apologetic purpose, stressing the reality of the empty tomb.

The importance of the resurrection claim for the early church cannot be overstated. While the Epistles present the cross as the core of our salvation, the preaching in Acts presents the resurrection as the core (2:24–36; 3:15; 4:10–12; 13:34–37; 17:31). We could say that Jesus' death is the theological core of our salvation, while his resurrection is the apologetic core. The cross and the empty tomb form a single event in salvation-history, and they are interdependent. In the preaching in Acts the apologetic aspect is primary, for the early church was trying to evangelize Jews and Gentiles. In 1 Corinthians 15 we see how critical the resurrection is for the New Testament message. There Paul is correcting a Hellenistic misunderstanding that there will be no resurrection; he responds by saying, "And if Christ has not been raised, our preaching is useless and so is your faith" (15:14). "Useless" (*kenē*) means "empty" or "of no value." In other words, Paul claims that Jesus' resurrection as a historical event is central to the Christian faith. Without the resurrection it is emptied of all value.

The Theories

All of us have to interact with the claim of resurrection. There are several theories regarding what happened historically. Scholars have suggested seven possible explanations of the evidence:

1. *The Conspiracy Theory.* In Matthew 28:11–15 we learn that the chief priests bribed the guards to spread the rumor that the disciples had actually stolen Jesus' body and made up the story of the resurrection. The resurrection would then be a hoax; it is likely that this was a widespread rumor among the Jews. Even the fourth-century historian Eusebius of Caesarea had to refute it, saying that followers of the high ethical standards of Jesus would hardly have perpetrated such a plot or invented such a falsehood. Why would they be willing to die for a blatant lie?[28]

2. *The Political Theory.* The earliest modern reinterpretation of the evidence came as part of the deist movement. H. S. Reimarus in the mid-eighteenth century gave a new twist to the conspiracy theory. He taught that the disciples made up the story to get celebrity and power for themselves. According to Reimarus, Jesus was a political opportunist who tried to start a messianic movement but died in the process. The disciples, wanting their own kingdom, stole the body and made up a story that Jesus was in heaven preparing to establish a future kingdom. Of course, Reimarus's theory suffers from the same weaknesses as does the conspiracy theory[29] and never gained many adherents.

3. *The Swoon Theory.* The rationalists in the early part of the nineteenth century tried to explain the biblical miracles as products of natural causes. For instance, the healing miracles were

due to the power of Jesus' personality, which convinced people they could be healed; Jesus' walking in the shallows early one morning looked to the disciples like walking on water; the feeding of the five thousand was the result of Jesus' talking a little boy into sharing his lunch—everyone else started sharing their lunches. According to Heinrich Paulus, Friedrich Schleiermacher, and Karl von Hase, Jesus swooned on the cross, and the guards thought he was dead. Jesus awoke in the tomb, escaped, and told his followers that he had been raised from the dead. This theory has been very influential and is similar to Muhammad's view that Jesus went to Kashmir after his escape and preached Islam there for forty years. His tomb is a holy shrine in Kashmir to this day. David Strauss showed how weak this theory is. No one who had suffered such massive physical trauma on a Roman cross could have survived. The Romans were experts at crucifixion and death. Their stabbing Jesus with a spear was to ensure his death. Medical experts tell us that the mixture of blood and water pouring out of the stab wound was evidence that death had already occurred.[30]

4. *The Mythical View.* In the middle of the nineteenth century Strauss developed one of the most influential explanations, that the stories of Jesus' miracles (including the resurrection) were not based on fact at all, but were legends or myths patterned after Greco-Roman and other myths of the ancient world. Strauss refuted the rationalist approaches once for all, for he said that they still made the miracles historical events. For him there were no events behind the accounts of miracles. They were created stories, legends that made the human Jesus a supernatural person. Thus they never happened! There never was an empty tomb or any postdeath appearances; at most there were hallucinations after the legend began circulating (hallucinations would explain passages like 1 Cor. 15:5–8). Many modern skeptics have followed in Strauss's train (e.g., Rudolf Bultmann, Paul Tillich, Alfred Loisy, John Crossan).

However, there are also great problems with this position: (a) There was not sufficient time for such a myth to develop; in all of history, no myth has developed in less than a couple of centuries. Yet we know on the basis of 1 Corinthians 15:3–5 that the story of the resurrection was already being told within ten years of the event. (b) Would the disciples have risked their lives and surrendered their futures on something they knew to be a myth? That is very doubtful. (c) The whole tone of the resurrection stories differs radically from pagan myths. The emphasis on eyewitnesses, the empirical and apologetic elements in the stories, and their realistic nature set these narratives apart. (d) Far from needing to be "demythologized" (Bultmann's term for the removal of supernatural myth from the Bible), the New Testament records had themselves actually demythologized certain Hellenistic myths by making them history! Some stories like the Emmaus Road incident and the miraculous catch of fish have parallels in Greco-Roman myth. They would have said to the ancient person, "Look, what you knew as legend has now come true! Jesus has done these things in real history."

5. *The Subjective Vision Theory.* Several scholars (Ernest Renan, Willi Marxsen, Reginald Fuller, to some extent also Strauss) believe that the disciples had a series of dreams about Jesus' being alive. These dreams became the basis of the resurrection stories. The problem with this view is that Jesus appeared to several who were not believers and were not expecting to see him alive (like his brother James and Paul himself). The disciples were a defeated, totally discouraged group after the crucifixion. It is highly unlikely that any mere dream could have turned them around, let alone effected the conversion of a convinced unbeliever like James or of an adamant opponent like Paul. Moreover, psychological theory cannot explain why such dreams continued for only a short time and then ceased, nor how such a dream could have been experienced by five hundred people at

the same time, most of whom, according to 1 Corinthians 15:6, were still around to testify!

6. *The Objective Vision Theory.* Still other recent scholars (e.g., C. F. D. Moule, Gunther Bornkamm, W. D. Davies, Edward Schillebeeckx) consider the appearances to be visions sent from God rather than mere dreams. God sent these visions to tell the disciples that Jesus' resurrection was a spiritual reality; while the event itself is not physically provable, the experiences of the disciples can be affirmed. The key is the word *ōphthē* (appeared) in 1 Corinthians 15:5–8; a form of the Greek verb "to see," it is here interpreted as a reference to seeing a vision rather than to literal sight. However, the rest of 1 Corinthians 15 looks at the transformation of the physical body into a spiritual body, and it is very difficult to conceive how a vision could relate to that transformed body. Furthermore, in 2 Corinthians 12 Paul carefully distinguishes between a space-time event and a vision; if the appearances in 1 Corinthians 15:5–8 were visions, Paul would have said so.

7. *The Corporeal Resurrection View.* The only remaining possibility is that Jesus physically rose from the dead. Several arguments have been raised against this view, and we will respond to each in turn:

a. Emphasis on a physical resurrection appears only in the later Gospels (Luke, John). However, while there is no corresponding emphasis in Mark and Matthew, there is such an emphasis in 1 Corinthians 15:3–8 (especially the appearance to five hundred at once) and 15:14–54 (the transformation of the physical body). The same is true of 2 Corinthians 5:1–8 (the heavenly tent that will clothe our mortal bodies) and 1 Thessalonians 4:13–18 (at the final resurrection we will meet our departed loved ones in the air). What these verses describe would be unlikely in anything but a physical resurrection.

b. In 1 Corinthians 15:8 Paul equates the other postresurrection appearances with his own Damascus Road vision. However, Paul is not really saying that his vision was the same type of experience as the appearances to the others. Rather, he is saying that his vision had the same impact on him that the others' experience had on them. True, in the vision the risen Lord revealed himself to Paul and, as with James (15:7), brought about conversion. But it goes too far to assume that the other appearances were also visions.

c. The appearances are related in mythological language. But we have already noted the differences between the appearance narratives and pagan myths. In the resurrection stories we have realistic narrative. The only people who see them as legends are those with an antisupernatural bias.

d. There are no analogical parallels in history for the resurrection, so it cannot be verified. Actually, there have been reports of resuscitation miracles (e.g., in Indonesia and China) in recent years. Miracles are alive and well on planet Earth. God is still in control, and his power is evident for those who have eyes to see and ears to hear. The real question is whether we are open to see and believe. In short, analogical parallels are available, though certainly not for the final resurrection. The question, then, is whether we have faith. The biblical record is certain, and the evidence is sufficient. Will we believe it?

Yet there are still problems. Although a good case has been made that Jesus' physical resurrection in space and time is likelier than the other options, doubts still remain. One of the biggest obstacles is the resurrection narratives themselves. Scholars have long noted the discrepancies in the accounts. Reading about the resurrection in the four Gospels is like discovering four different events, so pervasive are the differences. Mark, Luke, and John 20 relate Jerusalem appearances, Matthew and John 21 Galilean appearances. If Jesus appeared first in Jerusalem, why did the angel command the disciples to go to Galilee? Also, was there one angel (Mark, Matthew) or two (Luke, John) at the tomb? Were the angelic message and the appearance of Jesus for the women (Synoptic Gospels) or for Mary Magdalene alone (John)?

The solution for most evangelicals is to harmonize the accounts. However, this is highly debated, and many scholars believe that any attempt to harmonize is a denial of the autonomy of the individual Gospels. For a time that was my belief, but now I find such skepticism to be an overreaction and completely unnecessary. Harmonization of disparate witnesses is a critical tool for all historical studies. The only real question is whether it is done correctly. Certainly, shallow harmonization is often done (e.g., Tatian harmonized the Gospels by stringing them together into one long gospel he called the *Diatessaron*). However, critical harmonization that takes account of the tensions and seeks the most probable whole is mandated by deep historical study. The key is not to press the unity too far, but to let the evidence speak for itself.[31]

With this in mind, let me attempt to harmonize the empty-tomb and resurrection accounts in the four Gospels.[32] Near dawn on the first day of the week about thirty-six hours after Jesus' death, an earthquake occurred, and an angel appeared, rolling away the stone from the tomb; the guards fainted (Matt. 28:2–4). Just before dawn, several women had started for the tomb, planning to anoint Jesus' body with oil; they found the stone rolled away (Matt. 28:1; Mark 16:1–4; John 20:1). Mary Magdalene immediately ran and told Peter and John, who set out running to the tomb (John 20:2–4). In the meantime, James's mother Mary and Salome, still confused, entered the tomb and saw angels (there were probably two, with Mark mentioning only one for dramatic purposes) who told them of the resurrection and gave them a message that Jesus would meet the disciples in Galilee (Matt. 28:5–7; Mark 16:5–7). As the women left, they were filled with fear and speechless (Mark 16:8), but on the way Jesus met them and repeated the angelic message (Matt. 28:9–10). The women went to the disciples with joy, but the disciples didn't believe their report (Luke 24:10–11; cf. Matt. 28:17). Meanwhile, Peter and John had entered the tomb, with Peter going away confused (John 20:6–7; Luke 24:12) and John believing (John 20:8–9). Mary Magdalene had followed them and stood there weeping; she was met first by the angels and then by Jesus (John 20:11–17). Believing, she too returned to the disciples with the joyful report (John 20:18; Mark 16:10), but again they didn't believe (Mark 16:11). In the resurrection narratives, this concludes the empty-tomb accounts.

The appearance accounts are complicated by the Jerusalem and Galilee settings. Yet the disparity is not as great as at first appears. The disciples would naturally stay in Jerusalem for the Passover celebration before returning to Galilee, so it makes sense that the first appearances would be there. The command to go to Galilee was theological in intent and did not necessitate an immediate departure. My own belief is that there was a longer message, and that Mark and Matthew reported the Galilee command because of their own emphasis on the Galilee appearances. It has long been known that the Evangelists selected highlights from and summarized the messages of Jesus;[33] it is likely, then, that Mark selected what fit his emphases (cf. Mark 14:28 and 16:7). We conclude that Jesus told the women that he would meet the disciples in Galilee but did not say to go there immediately. So they stayed in Jerusalem for the feast days, and Jesus first appeared to them there.

The first appearance to the disciples may well have been to Peter, probably involving a private time of repentance, forgiveness, and reinstatement (1 Cor. 15:5). Then Jesus appeared to the two disciples on the road to Emmaus, eventually making himself known through the opening of the Word and the breaking of bread (Luke 24:13–32). They returned to the Eleven and reported with joy, and at that time Jesus appeared to the assembly (minus Thomas) and quieted their fears, telling them to wait for power from on high (Luke 24:33–49; John 20:19–23; 1 Cor.

15:5). A week later at the end of the Feast of Unleavened Bread (part of the eight-day Passover celebration), Jesus appeared to the Eleven again (with Thomas present) and gave final proof that it was he (John 20:26–29). After the feast the disciples returned home to Galilee, and while waiting for something to happen took up once again what had been the occupation of some of them, fishing. Jesus met them and gave them a miraculous catch of fish (John 21:1–14), this time reinstating Peter publicly (John 21:15–17) and prophesying his death (John 21:18–23). Some time later Jesus gave the disciples the Great Commission on a Galilean mountain (Matt. 28:16–20) and then appeared to over five hundred followers at the same time (1 Cor. 15:6). Next he appeared to (and converted) his brother James (1 Cor. 15:7). Finally he appeared to the Eleven near Bethany, blessed them (Luke 24:50; 1 Cor. 15:7; Acts 1:4–8), and then was taken from them in a cloud (Luke 24:51–52; Acts 1:9–11).

Of course, no harmonization can claim to be absolutely accurate, for we are trying to draw together four different narratives that had little interest in the chronology of the appearances as a whole. From Acts 1:3 we know that Jesus appeared to his followers over a period of forty days, and it is likely that there are several appearances that we know nothing about. It will be great to get to heaven and order the cassettes of that period to fill in the details! Until then we will go with the revealed accounts and trust that they are accurate. However, our harmonization does demonstrate that the so-called discrepancies are not insoluble and need not make us doubt the historical veracity of the four accounts.

In conclusion, we are now in a position to say that the evidence, honestly analyzed, points to a great likelihood that Jesus was indeed raised from the dead, and that this can be (indeed, has been) verified historically. The other options are not nearly as likely, for they cannot account for all the data, like how a dispirited, defeated rabble like the Twelve could not only be turned around into a joyous, victorious group, but changed into a band of charismatic apostles who would turn the world around and begin a process that would virtually defeat the Roman Empire for Christ! Moreover, if the writers were making up a story, would they choose as their first witnesses a group of women who by Jewish law could not be official witnesses? Very unlikely! No, the only possible explanation is that Jesus was raised from the dead and appeared over a period of forty days to his followers, changing them into a force that would evangelize the world.

THE IMPLICATIONS OF THE RESURRECTION FOR JESUS' OWN CLAIMS

Having shown the extreme likelihood of the resurrection, we now have to look more closely at what Jesus said about himself, his relationship with the Father, and God's Word. It is very clear that Jesus considered himself to be the Messiah, the Son of God (Mark 1:1). Ben Meyer has shown that this can be seen not only in his words but in his deeds as well. Jesus did not act like someone who thought of himself as merely a good teacher or prophet. The authority he evidenced, the way he related to his followers, to the crowds, and to the leaders, shows that he thought of himself as God.[34] His actual claims also bear this out. In the oldest Gospel, Mark, he implicitly accepts the titles "Holy One of God" (1:24) and "Son of God" (3:11) from the demons and "Messiah" (8:29) from Peter; then in 12:35–37 he uses Psalm 110:1 to say that he is greater than the "son of David"; and in 14:62 he declares not only that he is "the Christ, the Son of the Blessed One," but also that the high priest "will see the Son of Man sitting at the right hand of the Mighty One and coming on the clouds of heaven." The fourth Gospel contains the greatest claims, namely the "I AM" statements that equate Jesus with Yahweh. Included here are the absolute expressions in 6:20 and 18:5, the predicative sayings in 6:35 ("I am the bread of life") and 8:12 ("I am the light of the world"), and the direct claims of deity in 8:58 ("before Abraham was born, I am!"), in 10:30 ("I and the Father are one"), and in 10:38 ("understand that the Father is in me, and I in the Father").

And what of the Bible? Is it the Word of God? Here again Jesus was clear. He often identified Old Testament citations as what "God said" (Matt. 19:5) or as the "word of God" (Mark 7:9–13), and he was continuously quoting the Old Testament Scriptures as inspired truth with final authority. He also considered the events of the Old Testament to be historical. For instance, he placed Jonah's sojourn in the great fish on the same level as his own resurrection (Matt. 12:40). Inasmuch as the One who is very God himself continually anchored his arguments in Old Testament proof-texts, they have to carry a great deal of weight. In short, Jesus considered the Old Testament to be the Word of God; and in light of his resurrection and the validity of his claims for himself, we as well must consider it to be the Word of God. Jesus verified the claims of 2 Timothy 3:16–17 and 2 Peter 1:20–21 (see pp. 30–31), and so we too can accept the Bible as infallible.

3. The Reliability of the Process Establishing the Canon

We have demonstrated that the Bible is the Word of God. Yet how do we know which books are inspired? How did they come to be regarded as canon? The term *canon* originally meant "reed" and then came to mean, in succession, "measuring rod," "standard" or "norm," and finally "list" or "table." In the patristic period the term was used for the standard ethical and doctrinal content of Christianity, and since the fourth century has stood for the closed list or collection of authentic books in Scripture. Recently a large number of writings have probed various related issues, such as the status of the Apocrypha, the formation of the Old Testament canon, and debates in the early church on the subject. Let's look at the Old Testament, the Apocrypha, and the New Testament in order to evaluate the validity of the list of sixty-six books that make up our canon. Of course, the decisions of the early church as to which books are canonical are not inerrant in the same way the words of Scripture are. Martin Luther was within his rights to question James as "a right strawy epistle," although those who say he wanted it removed from the canon are wrong.[35] We believe that God guided the process, but there are no biblical claims behind the formation of the canon. So we need to work with the canon and authenticate the books for ourselves. Of course, we are helped by two thousand years of church history in which these works have been authenticated again and again. David Dunbar is correct when he says that the formation of the canon was a salvation-historical decision. So then, as we realize that God himself guided the process, we can work with the knowledge that the process was adequate and the received canon is closed.[36] In other words, whenever we come to individual books, we can be assured anew that the process was indeed from God. Now let us see how the process developed.

The New Testament quotes or alludes to nearly all the Old Testament books (though not quoted, Joshua, Judges, and Ezekiel are alluded to; Zephaniah, Obadiah, and Nahum are neither cited nor alluded to), citing them as Scripture. But when citing other works, such as 1 Enoch (Jude 14–15) or the Hellenistic philosophers (Acts 17), the New Testament never uses the term *Scripture*. When Jesus speaks of the martyrs from Abel to Zechariah son of Berakiah (Matt. 23:35), he likely is not speaking chronologically, since Uriah (Jer. 26:20–23) was martyred after Zechariah. Most likely, Jesus is referring to the canon, since Zechariah is mentioned in 2 Chronicles 24:20–22, the last book in the Hebrew canon. This may be evidence that the New Testament accepted a closed canon.

The Old Testament canon developed probably in two stages. The Law/Torah was recognized quite early, at least by the time of Ezra. We don't know when the collection of the Prophets and

Writings began, but probably it was linked to the growing realization that the age of the prophets had ceased. We also don't know when the books were divided into the Prophets and Writings, but the division was common by the end of the second century B.C. (it is mentioned in Sirach). Certain books like Esther, Song of Songs, and Ecclesiastes continued to be debated, but they were generally accepted. Scholars differ regarding the date by which the canonical decisions were made, with some arguing for closure as early as 200 B.C. and others as late as the end of the first century A.D. One thing we can know with a fair degree of certainty—by the time of the New Testament writings, the Old Testament canon was complete.[37]

But what of the Apocrypha?[38] Some scholars have held that while the Torah and the Prophets were a closed canon, the Writings were open and in some circles included the Apocrypha. However, most now agree that the works in the Apocrypha were not regarded as canonical in the first century, but were accorded a secondary status as having value for edification. In the Jewish world they were listed with the canon as being worthy of reflection. At Qumran (the source of the Dead Sea Scrolls) the Torah and the Prophets were considered canonical, but the Prophets probably included most of what the Hebrew canon called the Writings. The Apocrypha does not seem to have been regarded as Scripture (only Tobit, Ecclesiasticus, and the Epistle of Jeremiah have been found at Qumran). Later Christian scribes, apparently unaware of the Jewish opinions, began listing the Apocrypha with the canon. In Roman Catholicism, Augustine argued for including these works in the canon, while Jerome favored the Jewish canon, labeling them "apocryphal" or "hidden," meaning they were not part of the canon. Augustine carried the day, and they became part of the Roman Catholic canon, though they were considered deuterocanonical or secondary to the Old and New Testaments. The canonical status of the Apocrypha was later reversed by the Reformers. In light of the evidence that the Apocrypha was nowhere accorded canonical status in the first century, the Reformers' decision was the correct one.[39]

The process by which the New Testament canon was recognized is just as complex as that by which the Old Testament was recognized. We have no evidence of a canonical consciousness on the part of the writers themselves, though we theorized earlier (pp. 28–30) that three preliminary stages took place in the New Testament period—the Logia Jesu, the creeds and hymns of the early church, and the collection of Paul's epistles. Yet even though the New Testament authors had no consciousness of canonicity, they did write with apostolic authority and expected the churches to heed and obey their teachings. Moreover, they expected the churches to read their letters in public services and to pass them on to other churches (Col. 4:16; 1 Thess. 5:27; Rev. 1:3). I would also add a fourth stage, although we have no direct evidence—the recognition of the four Gospels. We don't know when they were collected (the first direct evidence is Tatian's *Diatessaron* in the middle of the second century), but from the start they were accorded a status above other lives of Christ. In short, there is sufficient evidence to believe that the canonization process began in the first century.

Immediately following the New Testament period come the writings of the apostolic fathers (1 Clement, Ignatius of Antioch, Polycarp, Didache, Epistle of Barnabas), taking us to the middle of the second century. In the early works (1 Clement, Ignatius) there is a certain authority attributed to the New Testament writings, but they are not called Scripture. In the later works, however, Paul's epistles and the Gospels are labeled Scripture and placed alongside the Old Testament. The first actual collection of a canon was done by Marcion, whose Syrian dualism led him to reject the Old Testament and those New Testament writings that he felt contributed to the Judaizing error. His canon consisted of the Pauline Epistles (without the Pastorals) and a reworked edition of Luke (minus all Jewish elements).

Marcion and the Gnostic heretics gave impetus to the need for a set of authoritative (canonical) documents to offset the false teaching. Justin Martyr, Irenaeus, and Tertullian in the latter half of the second century quoted the New Testament documents frequently as Holy Scripture. The principle of apostolic authority was developed to counter the prestige of false teachers, for instance, the Montanist movement, which arose about A.D. 160 and argued that its own prophecy was inspired and held the highest level of authority. Anti-Montanist writings developed the concept of a closed canon to offset such teaching. The Muratorian Canon (about A.D. 200) was the first orthodox list of New Testament writings. This list is fragmentary, so it is difficult to conclude too much about those works not mentioned. The four Gospels are apparently accepted (Matthew and Mark are not mentioned, but Luke and John are called the third and fourth Gospels), as are the Pauline corpus, two Johannine epistles, Jude, and apocalypses of John and Peter (with some churches refusing to read the latter). The epistles to the Laodiceans and the Alexandrians (Hebrews?) are rejected as Marcionite. The major criterion appears to be the universal practice of the church. Those works widely accepted are authoritative.

By the end of the third century a pattern had emerged. The four Gospels, Acts, and the Pauline corpus were accepted, but the Catholic Epistles and Revelation were disputed. The Alexandrian fathers of the third century (Clement, Origen, Dionysius) exemplify this pattern. Origen lists as disputed works Hebrews (though he personally accepted it), 2 Peter, 2 and 3 John, James, and Jude. Early in the fourth century, the great historian Eusebius of Caesarea offered a threefold classification: (1) recognized books (the four Gospels, Acts, fourteen Pauline books [including Hebrews], 1 Peter, 1 John, and perhaps Revelation); (2) disputed books (James, Jude, 2 Peter, 2 and 3 John); and

(3) nongenuine books (Acts of Paul, Shepherd of Hermas, Apocalypse of Peter, Epistle of Barnabas, Didache, and perhaps Revelation). The Cheltenham Canon, from the mid-fourth century, accepts all but Hebrews, James, and Jude. Athanasius, bishop of Alexandria, in his Easter letter of A.D. 367, became the first to list the twenty-seven books now held to be the New Testament. The councils of the late fourth and fifth centuries finalized the canonical decisions. The Council of Laodicea (363) followed Eastern church precedent by accepting all but Revelation. The councils of Hippo (393) and Carthage (397) accepted all twenty-seven.

Three principles became the criteria by which canonical decisions were made by the early church: (1) To be accepted as canonical, a book had to exhibit apostolicity, that is, it had to be written either by an apostle or by someone connected with an apostle (as Mark was with Peter, and Luke with Paul). (2) It had to be accepted by all orthodox churches or by the vast majority of churches. (3) It had to contain orthodox dogma as determined by the rule of faith or standard church doctrine.

At first glance, the reader might think that this historical survey denigrates the authority of the New Testament canon, since it took so long for canonicity to be finalized, and since so many of the Catholic Epistles (and Revelation) were disputed. However, that is not really the case. Considering the extent to which each book was read in large segments of the church and quoted or alluded to by early writers, each was indeed accorded recognition from an early date. Hebrews and James, for instance, were alluded to in 1 Clement, the very first of the extracanonical writings; and 2 Peter, the most disputed of the books, seems to have been accepted in the Eastern church by A.D. 200.

We can conclude that the process by which canonical decisions were made was not only adequate but divinely controlled. As Dunbar says so well:

The early church fathers show no consciousness that they are acting to establish the canon. Indeed, the very shape of the New Testament canon was securely fixed long before any fourth-century councils declared themselves on the matter. . . . The apparently spontaneous development of the (New Testament) canon suggests that it is more appropriate to speak of a *recognition* rather than a selection of the New Testament books, and that the same interpretation can be extended to the recognition of the Old Testament.[40]

In other words, God had already inspired the books, and the canonical decisions simply recognized that fact. Canon is not the same as Scripture; rather, it simply distinguishes those books God has inspired from those he has not (we might say the latter group are "perspired" rather than "inspired"). Every time we meditate upon or teach those inspired books, God affirms their canonical status again and again. Is the canon closed? Yes, for two thousand years of church history has proven that the decisions made by the councils were correct, and we can trust them. We can be certain which books were indeed the inspired Word of God, and which were not.

4. The Contribution of Text Criticism

We have concluded that the Bible is Scripture, the Word of God, and consists of the sixty-six books in the Old Testament and New Testament canons. However, we still have not established which version is the inspired Word. Is the person who says, "If the King James Version was good enough for the apostle Paul, it's good enough for me," correct? The task of text criticism is to decide the actual words of the inspired authors and therefore of the inspired text. Text critics compare the more than five thousand extant Greek manuscripts, quotes of Scripture in the church fathers, and the early versions to try to decide which readings represent the actual words of the authors. For instance, they try to decide whether the longer ending of Mark (16:9–20) was penned by Mark himself. Since the oldest manuscripts do not have the longer ending, and since verses 9–20 do not fit the style of Mark as a whole or of verses 1–8 in particular, scholars have rightly concluded that they probably were added in the second century to supply an ending.

There are two basic rules in text criticism: accept the reading that has the best external evidence (i.e., represents the best manuscripts) and that best fits internally (i.e., best accounts for the other possible readings). All the manuscripts have been rated in terms of when they were produced and how innovative they are (i.e., whether they tend to add material to the text). They also have been placed in families, that is, groupings of manuscripts that exhibit the same types of tendencies. Scholars note which readings are presented by the more reliable manuscripts and found in more than one family. These are the more likely readings. Also, the reading that can explain the existence of the others is more likely. For instance, one of the versions of Philippians 3:16 is clumsy, reading, literally, "Only unto what we have attained, walk in the same." A lengthier version reads, "Only unto what we have attained, walk by the same rule, think the same thing." It is likely that later scribes tried to smooth out the difficulties in the former version by adding to it. The shorter version, then, is probably original and to be preferred.

Clearly, text criticism is a tool to help us ascertain the inspired Word of God. For teachers and preachers, however, Walter Liefeld's caution is helpful:

> Unless the Bible used by those in the congregation has a different reading from that used by the preacher, or has a footnote saying that there is a textual variant, it is probably best not to mention the uncertainty. If it seems necessary to introduce the matter, I would encourage that the preacher affirm every time this happens, that this does not affect the integrity of the orig-

inal and that no doctrine would be left unsupported if a favorite reading must be abandoned because of a more valid variant.[41]

5. Other Reasons for a High View of Scripture

We have sought to make a strong case for the evangelical view that the Bible is the inspired Word of God, revealed from on high and inerrant in the original autographs. Other arguments can be and have been given for a high view of the Bible as inspired Scripture. Let us consider a few of them to strengthen our case.

We begin with a development of our discussion of text criticism. As we have seen, there are over five thousand Greek manuscripts of the New Testament. From the first four hundred years after the writings of the New Testament, we have nearly forty papyrus fragments and five whole codices or books containing large portions of the New Testament. Josh McDowell compares this with the works of the great classical writers. Of the epistles of Pliny the Younger, we have only seven copies from the first seven hundred years after writing; of the works of Suetonius, eight copies from the first eight hundred years; of some of Tacitus's minor works, one copy from nine hundred years; of Julius Caesar's writings ten copies and of Tacitus's *Annals* twenty copies from a thousand years; and seven copies of Plato and ten of Aristophanes from twelve hundred years.[42] There is much better evidence for the New Testament—many more manuscripts and much closer to the time of writing (the earliest fragments are less than a century removed from the actual writing!). Moreover, most of the New Testament could be reconstructed from quotes in patristic sources, many of which date to within two hundred years of the original writing.

We do not have the same quality and number of manuscripts for the Old Testament, but what we do have is even more remarkable. The professional Jewish scribes kept their copies marvelously intact. These scribes counted the number of words and letters in each section and knew its middle word. The result was that they knew exactly where they were at all times and checked constantly to make certain no mistakes had occurred. Consequently, the Masoretic text, which was in process of development from the sixth to the ninth centuries, is extremely accurate, even more so than the Septuagint and the Qumran scrolls, which antedate it by centuries.

Archeology is a notorious double-edged sword. At times it supports, at other times it detracts from the evangelical cause. There are simply too many unknown factors archeologically (e.g., the location of the village of Emmaus [Luke 24:13]). However, it must be said that archeology has never disproven any biblical story, and there is apologetic value in a nuanced use of the discipline. For instance, William Ramsay was a famous historian-archeologist and confirmed agnostic who at the end of the nineteenth century set out to disprove the Book of Acts. The more he researched the background, however, the more he became convinced that Luke was one of the most accurate historians of antiquity. This conclusion led to Ramsay's conversion. Also, studies of seminomadic movements in the second millennium B.C. have confirmed the picture of the patriarchs in Genesis. William LaSor, David Hubbard, and Frederic Bush note five areas of agreement: (1) the names of the patriarchs are from the second millennium, not the first; (2) the record of Abraham's journey from Ur to Canaan fits what we know about the social and geographical conditions of the period; (3) the pastoral and nomadic life of the patriarchs fits the culture of that time; (4) the social and legal customs portrayed in Genesis are accurate for that period; and (5) the religious portrait fits, especially the emphasis on local shrines and God as the God of the clan rather than of sanctuaries (cf. the deities of the Canaanites).[43] All in all, archeology has tended to shore up belief in the accuracy of the Bible.

Problem Issues and Passages in the Bible

We have supported a high view of Scripture theoretically; now we must support it inductively as well by considering a representative list of problem issues (we will focus in particular on whether miracles are possible) and passages (i.e., passages that present ethical difficulties or that seem to contain errors). Dewey Beegle calls for us to jettison the doctrine of inerrancy on the grounds that the Bible contains errors. He calls for a more dynamic view of inspiration and authority: "The whole history of God's redemptive activity is one in which the Holy Spirit has worked through imperfect means, both men and women, without the means being a handicap. . . . In all essential matters of faith and practice, therefore, Scripture is authentic, accurate, and trustworthy."[44] Obviously, it is impossible in a work like this to consider every problem passage (some scholars have come up with as many as two thousand passages that seemingly contain errors). After examining the issue of miracles we will consider three sample problem passages from each Testament to demonstrate the basic trustworthiness of Scripture. With years of teaching and study behind me, I have yet to be convinced that there are errors in the Bible. I trust that this sample list will help the reader feel confident as well.

1. The Problem of Miracles

F. F. Bruce in his *New Testament Documents: Are They Reliable?* says, "Anyone who attempts to answer the question which forms the title of this book must recognize that for many readers it is precisely these miracle-stories which are the chief difficulty in the way of accepting the New Testament documents as reliable."[45] Rudolf Bultmann has summed up this skeptical modern view:

> The whole conception of the world which is presupposed in the preaching of Jesus . . . i.e. the conception of the world as being

structured in three stories, heaven, earth, and hell . . . we call mythological because it is different from the conception of the world which has been formed and developed by science. . . . In this modern conception of the world the cause-and-effect nexus is fundamental. . . . In any case, modern science does not believe that the course of nature can be interrupted, or so to speak, perforated, by supernatural powers.[46]

Bultmann's summation holds every bit as true today. The postmodern age we live in is characterized by pluralism, relativism, and a willingness to allow every conceivable view—except the evangelical one! Humans have for over three hundred years struggled with the concept of a supernatural reality. Nevertheless, as Bruce says, if one is open to the possibility that the biblical documents are reliable, one must by definition be open to the supernatural realm, for it is at the heart of the biblical worldview. Any consideration of the God of the Old Testament or Jesus in the New Testament will have to be open to the possibility of miraculous events, because they are treated as natural occurrences.

Is science really opposed to the possibility of the supernatural? A century ago that would have been true, for Newtonian physics accepted the rigid dictum that behind every effect there must be a cause observable to the senses (this Newtonian position was somewhat strange, given that Sir Isaac Newton was a convinced believer). With that perspective, it is no wonder that scientists were often atheistic. However, all that has changed. Since Albert Einstein's theory of relativity and Werner Heisenberg's uncertainty principle, science now views itself with a great deal more humility. No longer is science prescriptive, setting down rules for what may be believed or known. Now it is descriptive, simply observing and reporting on what appears to be the case. All scientists are aware that in a universe with quasars and black holes, every natural law may be broken. In such a universe there is room for the supernatural. In fact, an extraordinary phenomenon has taken place in university classrooms around the world. Now evangelical believers are most likely to be found in the science and medical departments, and it is the arts (literature, history, sociology) that have become the bastion of the agnostics and the atheists. It is no longer science that is the problem, but the prejudices of those who have bought into a worldview that has no room for God.

Unfortunately, those prejudices with no room for God are still firmly in control of the universities. Phillip Johnson says:

> Secularists employ a definition of rationality that allows no place for a supernatural Creator. . . . The contemporary academic world takes for granted a philosophy called scientific natural- ism. According to this philosophy, nature is "all there is," which is to say the cosmos is a closed system of material causes and effects that can never be influenced by anything outside of nature—like God—for existence.[47]

In other words, much of academia still holds a Newtonian view of reality in spite of the evidence. For them knowledge belongs to the empirical realm, and religious belief can never get beyond the realm of subjective ideas. Johnson characterizes the prevalent theory of evolution as "a creation story for the culture, a story that . . . tells us that we were created by blind and purposeless material processes rather than by a purposeful Creator who cares about what we do and what happens to us."[48] In other words, the theory is not so much based on objective evidence as it is another type of faith statement advanced by the secular culture. The debate, then, is not over facts but over views of reality, and in this post-Einsteinian age there is no longer any scientific reason to reject the possibility of the supernatural. In fact, as we argued in the section on the historicity of the resurrection, there is every reason to affirm the supernatural.

Since the days of the eighteenth-century Scottish philosopher David Hume, however, there has been a rigid bias against the possibility of miracles. In his essay "Of Miracles," Hume argued that even if a so-called miracle should occur, and proof for it be proffered, that proof would inevitably be insufficient, for it would stand against the greater proof that the laws of nature by definition exclude such things. Since a miracle is a violation of the laws of nature, and since the laws of nature cannot be violated, there can be no miracles. A naturalistic scientist would argue that an event that seems to violate natural law does not point to a supernatural God, but simply to the need for us to rework natural law. Underlying the belief in miracles is insufficient knowledge on our part, not a transcendent being at work.

This is the crux of the issue. Do miracles really violate or break the laws of nature? Winfried Corduan speaks of two types of miracles, the superseding miracle that seems to defy the laws of nature (e.g., raising the dead or stilling the storm) and the configuration miracle in which natural processes are utilized, but the timing points to supernatural origin (e.g., the winds that parted the Red Sea during the exodus). Both types are miracles, but the former is more directly contrary to natural law. Corduan defines a miracle as "an event so unusual that, given all the circumstances, the best explanation is that God intervened directly."[49] Not all so-called miracles deserve the title; the question is whether any can rightly be called miraculous or whether natural law makes miracles an impossibility. Corduan argues that we must examine all possible miracles (including those of the Bible) on the basis of the evidence to see if there is a probability of divine intervention.

We must also consider whether divine intervention would be a violation of natural law. This is very doubtful. If we posit a supernatural God who created the universe, then natural law is part of that creation, and God is still in charge. Any intervention he might make in nature can hardly be called a violation.

William Craig notes the three main contemporary definitions of natural law. The regularity theory looks at natural law not as a law at all, but as a description of what scientists observe in nature; in this view any event, no matter how miraculous it might seem, simply becomes part of the description. The nomic-necessity theory considers natural law to be a universal generalization that is based on experience and that tells us what can and what cannot happen in the world. Again, the miraculous would not be a violation, but would simply necessitate an expansion of the experience base to account for it. Finally, the causal-dispositions theory states that all of nature is disposed to act in certain ways and normally will behave accordingly. A miracle is not a violation here either, for when God intervenes contrary to the propensity of nature (e.g., in multiplying the loaves or stilling the storm), the normal disposition (of food or storms) still remains. Craig defines miracles as "naturally (or physically) impossible events, events which at certain times and places cannot be produced by the relevant causes."[50] Since God is the God of the impossible, miracles contravene natural laws but do not violate them. Their very impossibility points to divine intervention as the necessary cause.

Richard Swinburne states that no one can in an ultimate sense know what constitutes a natural law. "Laws," as science formulates them, can only "describe what happens in a regular and predictable way. When what happens is entirely . . . unpredictable, its occurrence is not something describable by natural laws."[51] Such an occurrence may involve superior laws, God's laws, which can intervene within reality as well as intersect from beyond the natural realm. Indeed, what is a law? It is simply the way things habitually occur. What habitually occurs within the human realm is not necessarily what habitually occurs within the divine realm. Thus if we change our view of natural law, the objection to miracles will cease.

If we redefine natural law as we have suggested, the only thing that could actually disprove the possibility of a miracle is not scientific law, but rejection of the God of the Bible. If atheism could actually prove that there is no God, then by definition there could be no miracle, since any unexplainable event would simply become a Star Trek-like intervention of a higher natural law. However, atheists have not proven that there is no God. Their position is every bit as much a faith statement as ours, and indeed (as we have attempted to show) has far less evidence than ours to back it up. Which is more likely, that all the complex and wonderful facets of this natural world occurred as random evolutionary developments of a world-machine, or that there is a creative force behind them? That this world is controlled by chance or by the God of the Bible? That the resurrection is a legend about a mythical God, or that it actually occurred within history?

A miracle can be either the imposition of a higher natural law (in which case it is a miracle of timing, a configuration miracle like the parting of the Red Sea) or an impossible event that cannot be explained by natural law (a superseding miracle like the raising of the dead). Arguments against the possibility of miracles are in the final analysis nearly always circular: Miracles cannot occur because they go beyond experience, and they go beyond experience because they do not occur. However, people *have* experienced the miraculous; their testimony is rejected on strictly rational grounds by those who deny the possibility of miracles—such things do not occur, so no such testimony is accepted![52]

What should be the relationship between science and Scripture? Each must take its proper place in the quest for knowledge. Arthur Holmes calls for an "interpretive realism" that considers science not as an exact description of reality, but as a theoretical construct that helps make nature understandable for us. Accordingly, science should not overstep its bounds and propound a worldview, but simply provide conceptual models that make nature intelligible. These models, which are to be judged on their coherence and ability to explain the way things appear, cannot attain final or absolute truth.[53] Religion also provides models to enhance our understanding, but has a universal range (which entails developing a worldview) and is confessional (centering on faith as well as reason), while science is limited (to sense knowledge) and neutral (descriptive of nature). The two should supplement one another. The current conflict is due not to the disciplines themselves, but to a priori principles applied from outside.[54] Science is not a metaphysical system; rather, religion should work with science in relation to the created world. The two inform one another, and together they describe God's relationship to his creation.

In short, there is no viable reason to reject the possibility of miracles, and on the basis of Jesus' resurrection every reason to affirm their validity. As I. T. Ramsey points out, science can do no more than say that miracles have no place in scientific language. Given its partial knowledge of the natural realm, science cannot say there are no miracles. Miracles belong to the metaphysical language of God's personal activity and so are valid objects for inquiry.[55] Miracles come from outside the natural order. They are divine interventions, but they do not violate or contradict natural law. C. S. Lewis argues that while miracles intersect from outside, they leave natural law intact. They do not invalidate it, for they are caused by the same God who created nature. By intersecting from outside the natural realm and therefore highlighting natural law, they actually emphasize the harmony of nature.[56]

2. Genocide (Deut. 7:1–5 et al.)

A long-standing problem is presented by passages like Deuteronomy 2:34; 7:1–5; 20:16–18; and 1 Samuel 15:18, which command the total annihilation of whole Canaanite

tribes—men, women, children, even animals! Especially after
the actions of Hitler and Stalin as well as the more recent atroc-
ities in Bosnia and Rwanda, it is difficult for us to think of a God
of love and compassion requiring such a thing. Genocide is difficult to justify. However, one has to understand the actual situation behind these passages. First, all these tribes were characterized by hatred of God and his people; they had committed
extremely violent crimes in opposing the work of God. In Genesis 15:16 God says that he is waiting, "for the sin of the Amor-
ites [Canaanites] has not yet reached its full measure," meaning
that the time of judgment has not arrived. This tells us that God
was actually patient in his judgment. Moreover, the tribes to be
annihilated were guilty of the most heinous crimes—child sacrifice, divination, rampant idolatry, religious prostitution. The
verb used in God's commands to Israel is *ḥāram,* meaning "to
devote to destruction." In other words, this was not genocide
but divine judgment against a people so corrupt and dangerous
they had to be wiped out completely. As Walter Kaiser says,
"When a nation starts burning children as a gift to the gods (Lev.
18:21) and practices sodomy, bestiality, and all sorts of loath-
some vices (Lev. 18:25, 27–30), the day of God's grace and mercy
has begun to run out."[57]

Second, several passages tell us that God's intent was not only
judgment but also protection for his people. Exodus 23:33 says,
"Do not let them live in your land, or they will cause you to sin
against me, because the worship of their gods will certainly be a
snare to you." The term *snare* is used occasionally to describe
the corrupting effect of the Canaanites. Deuteronomy 20:17–18
directs, "Completely destroy them . . . as the LORD your God
has commanded you. Otherwise, they will teach you to follow
all the detestable things they do in worshiping their gods, and
you will sin against the LORD your God." In fact, whenever Israel
had failed to carry out God's command of utter destruction, the

Canaanites who survived inevitably drew Israel into idolatry and immorality.

The command regarding the Canaanites is similar to Jesus' command in Matthew 18:7–9 regarding false teachers in the church, "If your hand or your foot causes you to sin, cut it off and throw it away" (the similar command in Matt. 5:29–30 concerns personal sin). In Matthew it is excommunication, but with the heinous sins of the Canaanites more drastic measures were necessary. However, the metaphor is apt in both cases. A gangrenous member must be amputated lest the body be destroyed.

In summation, the commands to destroy whole Canaanite tribes will be offensive only if the whole concept of divine justice offends. A person unable to accept the biblical teaching on eternal punishment will of necessity be offended by the passages we are discussing. However, once we understand the necessity of divine judgment, they will not be so difficult to accept. We must remember that God did not command that every Canaanite tribe be annihilated. In fact, the Torah commands that the Israelites give full rights to all Canaanites living among them (Num. 15:15, "The community is to have the same rules for you and for the alien living among you"). Only those tribes guilty of implacable opposition and terrible sins were to be eradicated.

3. "The Sun Stood Still" (Josh. 10:12–14)

Few biblical passages are so astounding as the account of the time God seemingly caused the sun and the moon to stand still for an entire day while Israel's army "avenged itself on its enemies." There are two primary interpretations, both viable. Many see here a literal twenty-four period in which the earth's rotation around the sun was stopped (or perhaps the rotation took forty-eight instead of twenty-four hours). Of course, God could indeed do such a thing. The problem many have with this scenario is its catastrophic results in terms of gravitational pull, tidal waves, and the like, but again God has the power to keep those things from happening as well. Another problem is that the legends of a long day in ancient Chinese and Hindu records and of the discovery by astronomers of a day missing from the records of the stars cannot be verified.

When one studies the story itself more closely, another option presents itself. A coalition of southern Canaanite kings attacks Gibeon, a powerful Canaanite city that has made a treaty with Joshua. When the city asks Joshua for help, the Israelites make an all-night march uphill from Gilgal twenty miles away, surprise the attacking army, and rout them. The enemy flees west to Beth Horon and then south into the plain of Aijalon. The first miracle occurs in verse 11, as the Lord hurls huge hailstones only upon the fleeing enemy, "and more of them died from the hailstones than were killed by the swords of the Israelites." It is then that Joshua commands the sun and moon to "stand still" so that Joshua's forces can avenge themselves on their enemies.

The key is the meaning of "the sun stood still." We must remember that Joshua's forces had made an all-night march into the mountains, defeated a large army, and then pursued them through the next day. Needless to say, the Israelites would have been at the end of their resources, but the hailstorm not only killed many of the enemy, but also gave Joshua's army a needed respite from the heat of the day. The verb *dôm* (v. 12) can mean not only "stand still," but also "be quiet"; hence many believe the miracle was not a cessation of the earth's rotation, but a "silencing" of the sun. That is, under the cloud cover of the hailstorm, the Israeli army was able to continue fighting without the strength-sapping effects of the sun.[58] So the miracle was one of darkness rather than daylight, and the men were rejuvenated to continue fighting until the battle was completely won.

In a very real sense both options are viable, and it is impossible to know for certain. I admit to being attracted to the latter, but I will not be surprised if when I get to heaven the more traditional option proves to be the correct one.

4. Youths Killed by Bears (2 Kings 2:23–24)

The story in 2 Kings 2:23–24 has caused as much offense to readers as any other in the Bible. On the surface, it seems a grouchy old man (Elisha) walking to Bethel was mocked by a group of "little children" (a translation found in some versions), and lost his temper. He called down curses upon these innocent children, and two bears came out of the woods and mauled forty-two of them!

However, a deeper look at the story in light of its language shows a quite different picture. The Hebrew term to describe the age of the mockers is used of Isaac as he was about to be sacrificed by his father in Genesis 22:12, Joseph at seventeen years of age in Genesis 37:2, and soldiers in 1 Kings 20:14–15. It does not mean a small child but a young person between twelve and thirty years of age.[59] Moreover, the youths' taunt was not innocent. "Baldhead" was a scornful epithet that demonstrated not innocent needling but a deep-seated contempt for this prophet of God. Many scholars believe it unlikely that Elisha was actually balding; rather, these youths were mocking the prophet in the strongest possible terms. Further, the verb "go on up" is the same verb used of Elijah's "going up" to heaven in a whirlwind in verse 11 of this same chapter. These youths are telling God's prophet to get out of there and go join Elijah in heaven. There is no place for him down on earth! In other words, the taunt is not innocent, nor is it addressed merely to Elisha. Rather, it is part of Israel's deep-seated rebellion against God and his prophets.

Elisha's reaction is not just a desire for vengeance. Rather, in keeping with the Torah he is calling down a covenant curse on these youths. This is in a very real sense an imprecatory prayer like those of David in the psalms (Pss. 12, 35, 52, 57–59, 69–70, 83, 109, 137, 140). These cries for vengeance have also produced consternation, but they too have been misunderstood. As

Gordon Fee and Douglas Stuart have pointed out, David and Elisha are actually heeding the pronouncement of Deuteronomy 32:35 (and Rom. 12:19 KJV), "Vengeance is mine; I will repay," and calling for judgment on the basis of the covenant curses in Deuteronomy 28:58–63, which make provision for the annihilation of God's (and his chosen leaders') enemies.[60] The appearance of the two bears in this sense is divine justice and follows the warning of Leviticus 26:21–22: "If you remain hostile toward me and refuse to listen to me, I will multiply your afflictions seven times over, as your sins deserve. I will send wild animals against you, and they will rob you of your children. . . ." As Kaiser points out, this was another of God's warnings intended to bring his people back from their apostasy: "Instead of demonstrating unleashed cruelty, the bear attack shows God trying repeatedly to bring his people back to himself through smaller judgments until the people's sin is too great and judgment must come full force."[61]

5. The Staff/No Staff Controversy (Mark 6:8–9 and Parallels)

The closest thing to an outright contradiction in the Gospels occurs in Mark 6:8–9 and its parallels. Whereas in Mark the disciples are instructed to take staff and sandals but nothing else on their missionary journey, in Matthew 10:10 and in Luke 9:3 and 10:4 they are told to take neither staff nor sandals on their journey. There are several possible solutions for this problem:[62]

a. The apparent contradictions are actually different ways of stating the same larger truth—that in mission one must depend on God for every necessity—and thus they exemplify the extent of the Evangelists' freedom in retelling the sayings of Jesus. Many, however, argue that this would be too much freedom.

b. Mark is speaking of the shepherd's crook, which is used for support in walking (so Jesus says to take it), while Matthew and Luke are speaking of the shepherd's club, which is used for protection against wild animals (so Jesus says not to take it). The problem here is twofold: the same Greek word is used for "staff" in all three Gospels, and this explanation still does not account for the prohibition of sandals.

c. Mark tells the disciples to "take" a staff, while Matthew tells them not to "procure" or "buy" one. So the disciples were allowed to take a staff but not to buy extras. The problem with this is that Luke 9:3, which is a prohibition, has the same verb as Mark and thus prohibits "taking" a staff.

d. Matthew and Luke are drawing their material from Q (a collection of Jesus' sayings comprising 250 verses common to Matthew and Luke but not found in Mark) rather than from Mark. This explanation is very viable, for we know from Luke that there was more than one mission (the mission of the Twelve in ch. 9 and of the seventy in ch. 10), and we know from Luke 22:35–36 that the instructions were temporary, restricted to each mission, rather than permanent. So Jesus was free to change the instructions from one occasion to the other.

e. Mark's "take staff and sandals" stems theologically from Exodus 12:11, where the Hebrews just before the exodus are told to take only staff and sandals on their journey, while Matthew's and Luke's "don't take staff and sandals" stems from instructions regarding the temple—staff and sandals were to be left outside, since the temple stood on holy ground. While this is somewhat speculative, it does explain the theological reasons why Jesus on one mission would say to take staff and sandals, and on another to leave them behind.

In short, there is no true contradiction, and a combination of options (d) and (e) explains well the seeming discrepancy.

*6. The Day of the Last Supper and the Crucifixion
(Mark 14:12–15 and Parallels; John 18:28)*

The Synoptics place the Last Supper on "the first day of the Feast of Unleavened Bread, when it was customary to sacrifice the Passover lamb" (Mark 14:12=Matt. 26:17 and Luke 22:7), while John 18:28 places Jesus' arrest, trial, and crucifixion on that day ("to avoid ceremonial uncleanness the Jews did not enter [Pilate's] palace; they wanted to be able to eat the Passover"). This is one of the most difficult problems of chronology in the New Testament. Several solutions have been suggested:

a. Some believe that either the Synoptic Gospels or John is wrong, but it is difficult to believe that such important events would be misconstrued. While this solution is possible, it should be discarded if other solutions are viable.

b. Some like Joachim Jeremias in *The Eucharistic Words of Jesus* believe the Last Supper was not a Passover celebration but a preparatory meal linked with the Passover, like a *kiddush* or prayer meal (for which there is little evidence before the fifth century), a *habhurah* or fellowship meal with paschal significance, or a Diaspora meal celebrated on the basis of a different calendar (see solution [c]).[63] This hypothesis is possible but still conflicts somewhat with the data, since the Last Supper is called a Passover meal in the Synoptic accounts.

c. Anne Jaubert in *The Date of the Last Supper* proposes that two calendars were used, the solar calendar followed by the Qumran community and a few others (notably the author of the Book of Jubilees), and the lunar calendar followed by the rest of Judaism.[64] She suggests that the Synoptics (and Jesus), following the solar calendar, placed the Last Supper on the day preceding the crucifixion, while John followed the lunar calendar and placed the Passover meal on the day of the crucifixion. However, there is little evidence that Jesus followed a sectarian calendar, or that sacrifices were offered in the temple on any day other than the official day (see Mark 14:12). Therefore, this proposal is unlikely.

d. The most likely view is that the Last Supper was indeed a Passover meal celebrated on Thursday evening. Yet how do we account for John 18:28, which indicates that the Jews would eat the Passover meal after Jesus' arrest? The answer is to be found in the close connection between the Passover and the Feast of Unleavened Bread, which fell on the seven days immediately following the Passover. They were so closely connected that the entire eight days were described as the Passover celebration. The meal referred to in John 18:28 was actually the *chagigah*, connected with the paschal sacrifices offered throughout the week (*pesaḥ* in Deut. 16:2 and 2 Chron. 35:7).[65] By viably harmonizing the Synoptic Gospels and John, this final option removes the seeming contradiction.

7. Jesus versus Paul and Hebrews on the Law (Matt. 5:17–20; Rom. 10:4; Heb. 8:13)

Another of the thorniest problems in New Testament study is the conflict between Jesus' avowal of the eternal validity of the Law and the depreciation of the Law in Paul and Hebrews. In Matthew 5:18 Jesus says, "Until heaven and earth disappear, not the smallest letter, not the least stroke of a pen, will by any means disappear from the Law," while in Romans 10:4 Paul says, "Christ is the end of the law," and Hebrews 8:13 states that in the new covenant God "has made the first one obsolete." In recent decades as much ink has been spilt on this issue as on any other. Books, articles, and collected essays by the dozen have tried to reconcile the attitudes of Jesus and Paul toward the Torah or Law, but no consensus has been reached. Obviously, it is beyond this short section to resolve the issue once and for all; all I can do is sketch my proposed solution.

The key to Jesus' view is the statement in Matthew 5:17, "Do not think that I have come to abolish the Law or the Prophets; I have not come to abolish them but to fulfill them." In what way did Jesus "fulfill" the Law, and how does that relate both to the teaching on its continuing validity in verse 18 and to the antitheses ("It has been said . . . but I tell you") in 5:21–48? The verb *plēroō* occurs sixteen times in Matthew, ten of which denote Jesus' fulfilment of Old Testament promises. Its meaning there, as Douglas Moo has said, is to show "how Jesus has 'filled up' the entire Old Testament, not only by accomplishing what it predicted but also by reenacting climactically Old Testament historical events (e.g., 2:15)."[66] Its meaning here is that Jesus has "filled up" or "raised to a higher plane" the Law of Moses. There are both continuity and discontinuity in Jesus' statement. In one sense, the Law continues in Jesus' "Torah of the Messiah." The Jews believed that when the Messiah came, he would bring the final Torah that would complete the first Torah. The Sermon on the Mount in Matthew 5–7 is that final Torah. The antitheses of 5:21–48 bring out the discontinuity. The Law does not continue intact in the new covenant, but continues in the sense that it has been fulfilled. We keep the Law when we keep Jesus' teachings.

Paul's teaching is actually similar to that of Jesus. He says in Romans 7:12 that "the law is holy" (cf. Gal. 3:21), and in 8:4 he talks of "the righteous requirements of the law." Yet at the same time he can say in Romans 6:14, "You are not under law," and in Galatians 3:23, "We were held prisoners by the law." There have been any number of theories about Jewish views of the Law and Paul's relationship to them. Perhaps the most influential theory is that of E. P. Sanders, who says the traditional Lutheran view has misunderstood first-century Judaism as a legalistic religion centered on works. Sanders argues in his *Paul and Palestinian Judaism* that the Jews never considered works as a means of "getting in" (God's salvation) but of "staying in."[67] The actual basis of salvation was thought to be election and covenant (Sanders labels this view "covenantal nomism"). Paul opposed this view that one was right with God merely by being Jewish and declared instead that one could be justified only by means of Christ.

Sanders for the most part rules the day in studies of Paul and the Law. However, a number of problems still remain. For example, Paul says in Romans 3:20 that "no one will be declared righteous . . . by observing the law." On the basis of Sanders's view it is hard to see why Paul would say this. While Sanders is certainly correct that works were more for "staying in" than "getting in," he overstates the absence of legalism in Judaism. The Jewish people were automatically children of God by virtue of being the children of Abraham. Therefore, their concept of salvation was entirely centered on "staying in." In that sense there was a distinct legalistic strain within Judaism, and Paul correctly perceived the problem associated with the emphasis on the works of the Law. Paul's view was that the Law could save only if one were to keep it perfectly. Moreover, its basic purpose was not to save but to point out sin and thereby to point to Christ (Gal. 3:19–4:7).[68]

For Paul, Christ is "the end of the law" (Rom. 10:4), which means he culminates or completes the Law (the idea is similar to Jesus' "fulfill" in Matthew) and perhaps is also the goal of the Law (Gal. 3). Here too there are both continuity and discontinuity. In Christ the Law continues in completed form, not as a set of legalistic requirements. In fact, Paul speaks of the Law's being fulfilled (Rom. 8:4; 13:8, 10; Gal. 5:14). As Moo says, "the Mosaic law points to Christ and is dethroned from its position of significance in mediating God's will to his people with the coming of Christ."[69]

Finally, Hebrews has the strongest statements in the New Testament on the cessation of the Law. The Law was merely a "shadow" of what was to come in Christ (10:1; see also 8:5) and could never make anything "perfect" (7:19). There was inherently something "wrong" with the first covenant (8:7), and therefore it was "obsolete," soon to "disappear" (8:13). Certainly the author looked at the Law negatively, but that was due to the problem behind the epistle, a group of Jewish Christians about to apostatize and return to Judaism. Therefore, Hebrews does not contradict Jesus and Paul, but emphasizes the discontinuity over the continuity because of the problem addressed in the epistle.

In short, there is no final contradiction between Jesus, Paul, and Hebrews on the place of the Law in God's plan. All agree that it pointed to Jesus and was fulfilled in him. Jesus primarily presented the continuity between the Law and the new covenant in him, Hebrews the discontinuity, and Paul aspects of each.

We have noted that there are many problematic passages in Scripture, but I am not convinced that any can be labeled errors. We have made a strong case for the complete reliability of the Bible as the Word of God. We support, then, a view of inerrancy, that the Bible is without errors. Of course, a final harmonization is impossible, for there are many ways to interpret the difficult passages we have examined. However, I would argue in legal terms both that there is reasonable doubt that these passages can be designated errors, and that the same can be said regarding the other so-called hard sayings in the Old and New Testaments.

Yet it is also important to realize that the Bible is more than reliable. It is the inspired Word of God, the only source of eternal truth. All other books are fallible, written by finite authors who are often wrong. The Bible is infallible, written by human authors who were inspired by the divine Author who knows exactly the truths we need for faith and conduct. There is nothing in life as important as committing oneself totally to this divine Author; the principles for doing so are found in the Bible. Therefore, a chapter on biblical reliability, as well as a doctrine of inerrancy, is not an end in itself, but must be intended to call people to the Word of God, and to demonstrate why it is so critical to center one's life on the Bible.

It is the height of foolishness to believe in something but do nothing about it. If I, knowing that someone had put a million dollars in a bank account for me, never took any money out to pay my bills, people would consider me to be crazy. How much more foolish is it to know that the Bible is the Word of God but never spend any time in it? It would be equally foolish to squander all that money by spending it on frivolities that do not last. Something similar happens when I treat the Word shallowly by never taking the time to understand it. If I believe in inerrancy but never take the time to study the Bible, I am de facto denying inerrancy by caring nothing about what God is saying in his Word. In other words, part of believing in a high view of Scripture entails determining what the divinely revealed message of Scripture is! The next two chapters probe these issues, how to discover the inspired meaning of the Bible, and how to develop our theology from the Bible.

Recommended Reading

Craig Blomberg. *The Historical Reliability of the Gospels.* Downers Grove, Ill.: InterVarsity, 1987. Must reading for anyone serious about the Gospels. This work was commissioned by Tyndale Fellowship in Cambridge, England, to summarize the *Gospel Perspectives* series and shows the historical reliability of the Gospels better than does any other work yet produced.

F. F. Bruce. *The New Testament Documents: Are They Reliable?* 5th ed. Grand Rapids: Eerdmans, 1960. Still the classic work on the reliability of the New Testament and must reading for anyone interested in the issue.

Earl Radmacher, ed. *Can We Trust the Bible?* Wheaton, Ill.: Tyndale, 1979. A series of stimulating articles on the issues discussed in this chapter.

Can We Understand the Bible?

Have you ever thought about participating in a hunt for buried treasure? Imagine being captain of your own vessel and preparing to dive into the deep green waters for the lost treasure ship of Blackbeard. Since the radar shows it to be ten thousand feet under the surface, you climb into the miniature submarine or submersible, taking a huge cable down into the lightless deeps. Your foray the day before revealed a massive (treasure?) chest resting on the bottom about a hundred yards from the ship. With the mechanical arms of the submersible, you try to attach the hook at the end of the cable to the chest, but it keeps slipping off. Again and again you try, but each time failure results. Sweat pours off your forehead, and your hands become slippery. Suddenly, you notice two brass handles on the chest that are still intact. The hook holds, and slowly the chest rises to the surface as you follow in the submersible. On the ship you wait with bated breath as your assistant opens the chest: the treasure is there! Suddenly you are rich and famous. Gold doubloons, pearl necklaces, priceless ancient coins unique in the world—all yours!

Imagine undertaking the same quest with no preparation—no map to guide you, no computer or radar to find the ship, no equipment for deep-sea diving. Only a rowboat, scuba gear, and a dream. That would be rather foolish, wouldn't it? We have all read about the massive expense and preparation of modern-day treasure hunters, for instance, those who found the *Titanic.* No one goes into such an enterprise without a great deal of knowledge and preparation.

Studying the Bible is the greatest treasure hunt in history, and as such Bible study also needs to be done with great care and precision. Finding Blackbeard's treasure would bring earthly riches that would last a while (actually a long while!), but they would eventually be gone. Studies of lottery winners have shown that sudden earthly wealth usually brings little true happiness. But eternal treasure from God's Word never fades away, and the joy it produces satisfies far more deeply. Yet like treasure hunts you get only as much out of Bible study as you put into it. The deeper you go into it, the more treasure you get out of it. A great English theologian of the nineteenth century was on his deathbed. In too much pain to sleep, he spent the night meditating on the Lord's Prayer. The next morning he told his family that at every point he was led beyond his depth. It is impossible to probe too deeply into the eternal treasures of the Bible.

Each of us must ask ourselves certain questions: How well do I want to know God? Is knowing God enough of a priority in my life that I am willing to take time out of my busy schedule to get to know him better? Do I care enough about his Word to make it central in my life? The fact is that the only place God has told about himself is in the Bible. Most of us realize this, of course. Bible-study groups are growing in numbers all the time, and sales of Bibles have never been higher. However, surveys have also shown that actual knowledge of the Bible is diminishing while sales are expanding. In other words, interest is rising, but knowledge is falling. The purpose of this chapter is to provide an antidote by teaching us how to dig for buried treasure. The tools are available for anyone who cares enough to acquire and use them, and the results in this case are guaranteed.

Why Do We Have to Interpret the Bible?

The process of studying the Bible is called "hermeneutics," a term that comes from the Greek word for "interpretation." The first and most important step in interpreting the Bible is actually to realize we are supposed to do so. At first glance this seems obvious: the Bible is God's Word, so shouldn't we seek God's meaning? But few of us have been trained to think this way. Most of us have a haphazard approach to Scripture. We spin our finger in the air, so to speak, letting it fall on the text we know not where. What we want is a thrill, that is, we want the text to touch our hearts somehow. In and of itself, this is not necessarily wrong, except that our "felt needs" too often take precedence over biblical truth.

The "memory verse" movement is an example of an inadequate approach to Scripture. In the past, verses were taken out of context; the impression was that once a verse was memorized, God would bless whatever we did with it. Recently, the emphasis has shifted to memorizing whole sections so as to learn context. This is a valuable step forward, for verses don't have meaning apart from context. But we need to go one more step forward, for only rarely is there an emphasis on studying the passage to find out what it *means*. The fact is that the best way to memorize a passage is to study it deeply. Then one learns not only the words but also the message. And not only that—the meaning discovered under the surface of the passage is always exciting and life-changing. And it is God's message!

Still, why do we need complicated modern methods for accomplishing what should be simple—understanding the Bible? Several arguments can be made against the focus of this chapter: first, we should rely on the Holy Spirit, not on human tech-

niques; second, the biblical writers themselves, when interpreting Scripture, did not use complicated methods, but focused on
the simple meaning of the text (one is reminded of Mark 1:22—
Jesus taught "as one who had authority, not as the teachers of
the law" [=seminary profs!]); third, throughout church history
Christians have done quite well without hermeneutics, so why
now? Each of these arguments is worthy of reply.

First, there is no passage in the Bible that says the Holy Spirit
will tell us the meaning of the text; rather, the Spirit uses the
text to convict us and draw us closer to God. The question is
not whether the Spirit can use what we come up with, but
whether we want to get to know God's Word more deeply.
Because it is God's Word, we ought to want to know God's meaning, that is, the meaning God inspired as the author wrote.

On the second issue, the New Testament writers' method for
interpreting the Old Testament was clearly not a set of modern
hermeneutical principles, but how could it be? In each biblical
era of interpretation (e.g., the prophets' interpretation of the
Torah or Law of Israel, and the later prophets' interpretation of
the earlier prophets), the writers used the methods of their own
times. This is called "divine accommodation," meaning that God
used the understanding current at the time to communicate his
revealed truths. Should we become first-century rabbis because
Jesus used their logic in passages like Mark 11:27–12:34 (debates
with the leaders in the temple)? Of course not! Nor should we
use rabbinic ways of interpreting the Bible just because the New
Testament writers did so. Rather, we use the methods of our day,
and God blesses them. Our goal is to understand the message of
the sacred text as well as we can, and we rejoice in anything that
will help us reach this goal.

On the surface the third criticism, which is actually an exten-
sion of the second argument, has merit. Consider, however, that
the understanding of hermeneutical techniques has developed
throughout church history, and each step forward increased the

church's knowledge of Scripture. In addition, none of the great men and women of God (e.g., Augustine, Thomas Aquinas, Luther, Calvin, Wesley) were satisfied, for all sought to learn more. The same is true today. The contents of this chapter do not constitute the ultimate development of the process of discovering God's message in his Word, but it is hoped that they will provide another step forward.

Still, many readers will ask, "But why all these complex stages? Isn't it enough to simply read the Bible and let it speak to me?" Two responses are necessary. First, in one sense it is enough, for a simple reading of God's Word has been profiting his people for centuries. But there are several levels of understanding—a basic devotional level, serious lay Bible study, the respective planes of Bible-study teachers, pastors, and scholars writing commentaries. Each level is used mightily by God. The question is whether we have to (or want to) remain always at the first level. This chapter affords the opportunity to raise one's sights to an exciting new level.

The second response is to ask whether a simple reading can in the final analysis suffice. The story is told of an earnest student who challenged a professor: "It is so hard for you to understand the Bible. I just read it and God shows me the meaning." But while the student's statement reflects "a commendable confidence in God, it reveals a simplistic (and potentially dangerous) understanding of the illumination of the Holy Spirit and the clarity of Scripture."[1] Reading a text inductively yields a basic level of understanding, but we cannot help understanding it on the basis of our own set of beliefs and experiences. We are inevitably limited by our own presuppositions. To go deeper into the understanding of the original author (as inspired by God), we need the tools of interpretation. The purpose of this chapter is to help the reader acquire and use these tools.

Finally, consider that the postmodernists, as we saw in the previous chapter, challenge the very possibility of ever discovering the original intended meaning of the Bible (indeed, of any book). They argue that every reader produces one's own understanding, and that the author no longer has a voice in the text. I agree that it is difficult to discover the original meaning, and that most people fail to do so but instead read their own meanings into the text. However, it is not impossible to identify the original meaning. This chapter will counter the skeptics and help the reader discover God's intended meaning in the biblical text.

The Basic Process of Serious Bible Study

The goal of serious Bible study is twofold—to discover the intended meaning of the passage, and to ascertain the significance of that meaning for our lives today. The intended meaning is the message God has given to his people through the divinely inspired author. In other words, it is the original author's meaning and God's inspired meaning at the same time. Amazingly, while we all believe this, we often fail to make the effort to discover exactly what God intends to say in a given passage. If we believe the Bible is inspired, the inspired message (not what we want the Bible to say) is the true goal of Bible study. Then the treasure we dig up is real gold and not fool's gold. Correspondingly, the value of the biblical text for our lives is linked to the extent to which we apply the meaning of the text itself rather than a meaning we impose upon the text. Each step away from the inspired text has less authority, so we must link our interpretation as closely to the text as we can, and link the application as closely to our interpretation as we can (for the different levels of scriptural authority see figure 1). The way to do this is through serious Bible study.

Figure 1
Levels of Authority

Level I	Text	Implicit Authority
Level II	Interpretation	Derived Authority
Level III	Application	Applied Authority

There are three approaches to good Bible study, and each is critical to a proper understanding of Scripture. The third-person approach asks, "What does *it* mean?" and treats the Bible as an object for study. The first-person approach asks, "What does it mean for *me?*" and uses the Bible for devotional input. The second-person approach asks, "What can the Bible mean for *you?*" and preaches or teaches the Bible. The key point is that the Bible must be studied at each of these levels and in this order, or great problems will result. If we treat the Bible only at the third-person level, we have a sterile message devoid of relevance for today; here we find the seminary prof who sits alone in an ivory tower. If we take only a first-person approach, the Bible becomes subjective, without truth content; here we find the Christian who, rather than seeking God's message, uses the Bible for one's own ends. If we take only the second-person approach, the Bible is used to manipulate others; here we find the preacher who makes the Bible a club to beat others over the head. The solution is to follow the proper order in studying the Bible: (1) study it to find out its inspired, originally intended message; (2) make personal application of that message; and (3) apply it to others. The Bible is meant to be directed toward our own life and then to be shared with those people whose lives we touch.

Another way to picture sound Bible study is via two technical terms. "Exegesis" comes from two Greek words meaning "to draw *(hēgeisthai)* out of *(ex)*" a text what it means, while "eisegesis" means to "read *(hēgeisthai)* into *(eis)*" a text what one wants it to mean. To understand the Bible requires exegesis, not eisegesis, to seek the text's true meaning rather than a meaning that fits one's own needs. When I was first married, I wanted to do something special for Nancy's birthday, so I decided to bake our favorite dessert, carrot cake, from scratch. However, I knew nothing about baking cakes, so I found myself making numerous phone calls asking women in our church what terms like "cream," "grease the pans," and "self-rising flour" meant. What would have happened if I had just guessed at the meanings and gone ahead with the cake? I shudder to think of the result! The actual result was one of my few culinary triumphs, but only because I found out what the words meant. Good Bible study demands a similar effort. In every area of life we are concerned with meaning. Shouldn't we be equally concerned with the meaning of the Bible?

If we make the effort to discover the meaning of Scripture, we will uncover unbelievably exciting truths. This is the point of our illustration of buried treasure. There are wondrous truths waiting to be uncovered by any believer willing to use the tools for digging out the golden nuggets of meaning under the surface of the text.

The process of Bible study has several elements—inductive, deductive, and applicational study. Inductive analysis is to move from the data to conclusions, that is, to study the text by itself in order to find meaning. Deductive analysis is to move from other people's conclusions back to the data, that is, to use study tools like commentaries, dictionaries, and atlases to understand the text more deeply. These two elements supplement each other, so neither should be used exclusively. Inductive study is very helpful, but if used as an end in itself, it can become quite subjective, since we cannot help reading twentieth-century meanings into the ancient words of the biblical text. Deductive study by itself becomes too academic and can lead to merely parroting the conclusions of various commentaries. The two should inform one another. Applicational analysis takes the results of inductive and deductive study and applies the meaning of the text directly to our lives today.

Preliminary Issues in Interpretation

Interpreting Scripture is a science, an art, and a spiritual act. As a science it demands and follows certain principles or rules.

As an art it requires a certain feel for the task, a facility that comes from experience. I tell my hermeneutics students that after ministering for a couple of years they will be able to prepare their sermons in half the time it takes them now; with experience comes an ability to make decisions and craft a sermon or Bible study far more easily. As a spiritual act Bible study constitutes worship and communion with the living God. God speaks to us as we read and study his Word.

The Holy Spirit is the essential force in a proper understanding of the Bible.[2] Everything we do depends upon the empowerment of the Holy Spirit, lest the flesh have precedence and our actions come to naught. This is especially true of Bible study as a spiritual act. As John Calvin has said, the internal witness of the Spirit both brings us to salvation and enables us to understand Scripture.[3] However, the role of the Holy Spirit has often been misunderstood. Many have thought that the Spirit tells us the meaning of the text, and so in some circles the use of commentaries and like aids has been thought a denial of the Holy Spirit; some have even gone up to the pulpit and waited for the Spirit to tell them the message to preach. But the term used of the Spirit's role in interpretation is "illumination"; this refers to the internal work of the Spirit as we study the Word of God. In other words, the Holy Spirit does not whisper to us the meaning of the Word, but opens our sinful hearts to the Word and uses the results of our study to change our lives. The Spirit guides our hermeneutical feet, so to speak, as we study the text, but this does not result in an automatic understanding of its original meaning; rather, he guides our Bible study toward its significance for our lives.

Paul constantly spoke of and prayed for the understanding and knowledge that come through the Spirit (1 Cor. 2:12; 2 Cor. 4:4–15; Eph. 1:17–19; Phil. 1:9–11; Col. 1:9–13); he meant not just proper interpretation, but the power of the gospel to change lives. In short, the Spirit uses the Bible to direct our lives;

thus he works with rather than replaces serious Bible study. Before we begin our study, the Spirit prepares our hearts and minds to be open to the truths found in the Word; during our study the Spirit uses our developing understanding to draw us to God and give us spiritual maturity. The Spirit does not give us complete understanding or ensure the accuracy of our conclusions. Individuals equally committed to God and open to the Spirit will continue to disagree on the meaning of specific texts.

One reason for different conclusions on the part of Spirit-filled interpreters is our respective preunderstandings, the set of beliefs and ideas we bring to the text. We gain our set of preconceived understandings from three sources—the tradition we grew up in (e.g., Lutheran, Baptist, Pentecostal, Mennonite); the community or church to which we now belong; and the experiences we have had. This set of presuppositions exerts tremendous influence as we read the text. In one sense our preunderstanding is our friend as it provides a means of comprehending the text and organizing our thoughts as we study. In another sense it can be a barrier to truth, leading us to manipulate the text to make it conform to our preconceived ideas. In other words, preunderstanding can become prejudice!

Let me give an example of the influence of preunderstanding. Suppose we are studying the doctrine of the security of the believer. We focus on passages in John (6:35–44; 10:27–29) that support eternal security and passages in Hebrews (6:4–9; 10:26–31) that speak of the possibility of losing one's salvation. Those of us who have grown up in Reformed or Baptist circles (more Calvinistic) will prefer the John passages, while those who have grown up in Wesleyan or Mennonite circles (more Arminian) will prefer the Hebrews passages. Both sides will use their favored passages to interpret the passages that challenge their views. The solution is to develop an open attitude with regard to our preformed views, that is, to allow the text to challenge and if necessary to change the views we presently hold. We must allow the data of the text to test and at times correct what we currently believe about the meaning of individual texts or of an accumulation of texts. In other words, we must work with our traditions on the basis of Scripture rather than work with Scripture on the basis of our traditions. It is the Word of God that must have the final say.

The way to make decisions about the meaning of particular texts is to examine the options and test each one to determine which best fits the context and language of the author. While we will make decisions on the basis of specific hermeneutical principles, we will also utilize a general approach that has been called "critical realism," by which we mean the belief that each text has a "real" meaning that can be "critically" tested or verified in terms of its truth content.[4] In other words, there is an original intended meaning, and through Bible study we can discover that meaning. Texts are not playgrounds on which we the readers can play whatever game we wish. To take this approach is to deny the possibility of absolute truth and to justify the twisted interpretations of every cult group. Rather, biblical texts are divinely inspired, and finding their inspired meaning is the goal of our study.

We can discover the meaning of biblical texts through critical examination and reflection. Certainly, Christians will continue to disagree, but this very disagreement helps us overcome the bias of our preunderstanding. Opposing interpretations drive us back to the text to reconsider whether our conclusion might be based not on the text itself, but on preconceived notions as to what the text *must* mean. Of course, we will find the meaning only if we take opposing views seriously and try to learn from them rather than just try to prove them wrong.

In returning to the text, we can test each competing interpretation through a series of criteria: (1) Does it fit the larger context in which the text is found and explain the whole passage better than do the other options (criterion of coherence)? (2)

Does this option account for all the data better than do the other options (criterion of comprehensiveness)? (3) Is the explanation more adequate than other possibilities; in other words, does it make more sense (criterion of adequacy)? (4) Does it fit the author's language and theology better than do the other options (criterion of consistency)? (5) Does the option have staying power, or is it only a flash in the pan that will probably not stand the test of time; in other words, does the larger community of scholars and the church affirm its viability (criterion of durability)? (6) Does this option accommodate many schools of thought and bridge several other possibilities (criterion of cross-fertilization)? These criteria will inform and be worked out in the principles of interpretation that we will discuss in this chapter.

Inductive Study of the Text

Inductive analysis is the first step in studying a biblical text; it involves the individual's wrestling with the text without any help from dictionaries, commentaries, and similar aids. Many excellent works have been written on inductive Bible study, all emphasizing that the key is to pay close attention to the text and observe its details.[5] The Bible must interpret itself, and all conclusions should be based on the nature of the scriptural text. The value of inductive analysis is that the Bible as the object of study and the reader as the interpreter of the text are central. The disadvantages are the absence of controls against subjective interpretations and the impossibility of getting back to the original meaning given by the author. Therefore, inductive study must be supplemented by deductive analysis, which adds the historical element missing in a purely inductive approach. As a result, many of the topics discussed in books on inductive Bible study (such as word meaning and literary forms) we will save for our discussion of deductive analysis, where commentaries, grammars, and other external tools are utilized. Here we will concern ourselves primarily with the structure and development of the individual biblical text. There are two aspects to inductive study—the charting or outlining of the book as a whole, and the charting of the individual paragraph.

It is important to realize that the Bible was not written with either verse or paragraph divisions. In 1551 a Parisian publisher named Robert Estienne (Stephanus) became the first to issue a Bible with verse and chapter divisions. He made the divisions himself during a six-month publicity tour for his latest Bible version. Tradition says the divisions were made while Stephanus was riding his horse. Because the horse's movements kept jostling Stephanus's pen, the divisions were done hastily and often poorly, but the work became so popular so quickly that no one dared change them afterwards. So we must ourselves determine the outline and paragraphs of a biblical book rather than trust what is there. It is wise, however, to begin with a version that is divided into paragraphs (like the NIV or NRSV). It is not critical at this stage to determine the exact paragraphs, for we seek an understanding of the whole book. The task here is to develop a map of the book as a whole. We will use Philippians as our model.

The best maps take the form of a chart organized chapter by chapter (see figure 2). The first step is to skim each paragraph in turn and summarize its contents in six to eight words. At this stage we look at the paragraph for no more than a couple of minutes (so as not to get bogged down in details) and then sum up the whole. We might summarize Philippians 1:3–8 as "thanksgiving (vv. 3–4) for fellowship (vv. 5–6) and sharing (vv. 7–8)," though "thanksgiving and joy (v. 4) for God's work in us (v. 6)" is also a possibility. Developing a map of the whole book section by section in this way is actually a lot of fun; in fact, when I conduct Bible-study seminars in churches or parachurch groups, this step excites people more than does any other part of the study.

After completing the whole book we go back and draw a line between those paragraphs where there is a major change of focus

Figure 2
Chart of Philippians

Ch. 1	Ch. 2	Ch. 3	Ch. 4
1–2 Salutation	1–4 Unity and humility rather than conceit	1–4a Warning against the Judaizers	1 Call to stand firm
3–8 Thanksgiving for fellowship and sharing	5–11 Christ's example in humiliation and exaltation	4b–6 Paul's greater credentials	2–3 Plea for harmony
9–11 Prayer for the Philippians' love and discernment	12–13 Responsibility and empowering from God	7–11 All loss to gain Christ	4–7 Exhortations to rejoice, be gentle, and pray concerning anxieties
12–14 Paul's imprisonment as advancing the gospel	14–18 The need to witness rather than complain and fight	12–14 Striving for more of Christ	8–9 Exhortation to think and do the right things
15–18a His rejoicing when his opponents preach	19–24 Timothy commended for his genuine interest	15–16 Call to heed	10–13 Joy and contentment in the Philippians' sharing and Christ's provision
18b–26 His continuing to rejoice whether freed or executed	25–30 Epaphroditus commended for risking his life	17–21 Contrast between true and false teachers	14–19 Joy and contentment explained further
27–30 Unity in spite of persecution			20–23 Doxology and closing greetings

or emphasis. Among the divisions in Philippians are the introductory prayer (1:3–11), Paul's discussion of his current situation (1:12–26), his discussion of unity and humility among the Philippians (2:1–11), their ethical responsibility before God (2:12–18), the commendation of Timothy and Epaphroditus (2:19–30), and the warning against the Judaizers (3:1–6). The next step is to read through the book a third time, drawing double lines at the major section breaks. The result will be a thorough outline comprising major sections (double lines), minor sections (single lines), and paragraphs. It is often surprising how close this outline comes to the outlines in the commentaries.

Mapping a smaller book can be done in thirty to forty minutes once one becomes used to the process. In larger books like

Isaiah or Matthew, it is best to proceed chapter by chapter rather than paragraph by paragraph. Otherwise, it will take far too long and be counterproductive. It is amazing how much a brief inductive analysis will help us understand even as complex a book as Revelation.

The first chapters of Revelation seem to progress via contrasting scenes. The picture of the heavenly Son of man walking among the lampstands (1:12–20) contrasts with the terrible problems of the seven churches (chs. 2–3), persecuted from without by the pagan Romans and constantly bombarded from within by cult groups. Chapters 4–5 are a further heavenly vision, the glorious throne room of the sovereign God, who is worshiped by the elders and living creatures (ch. 4), and the worthiness of the Lamb of God to open the seven seals of the scroll (ch. 5). In chapter 6 the seals of the heavenly scroll are opened, and judgments are poured out upon the earth dwellers. Chapter 7 is a contrast, an interlude between the sixth and seventh seal (8:1); the 144,000 saints are sealed and then the heavenly multitude worships God for vindicating the martyred saints. Chapters 8–9 return to the theme of judgment, as the seven trumpets are blown and disaster is poured out upon those who oppose God and his people. Noteworthy in these early chapters is the constant juxtaposition between heaven scenes (chs. 1, 4–5, 7) and earth scenes (chs. 2–3, 6, 8–9), with the heaven scenes centering upon worship, joy, peace, and vindication, and the earth scenes centering upon persecution, judgment, terror, and rejection. The one theme that draws these disparate scenes together is the sovereignty of God, which is the major theological emphasis of the book. God is in charge of both heaven and earth, and the rest of the book pictures him as drawing history inexorably to its final conclusion.

Chapters 10–14 provide two interludes. The first, which comes between the sixth and seventh trumpet, details the angel with the little scroll that is sweet in the mouth, but bitter in the

belly (ch. 10). This is followed by the account of the two witnesses who, having been triumphant over the earth dwellers, are
slain by the beast but then are caught up to heaven (ch. 11). The
second interlude is an interconnected series detailing the war of
the red dragon against God and his people. It begins in chapter
12 with the dragon pitted against the woman (the people of God)
and the child (the Messiah). Then the dragon sends two beasts
to carry out his war against God's people (ch. 13). Together they
form a false trinity (cf. 16:13). Chapter 14 provides a contrast
by showing the ineffectiveness of the dragon's war; after the victory song of the 144,000 (the very ones pursued by the beasts!),
three angels give warning of the judgment about to poured out
upon the beasts and their followers. This judgment is detailed
in the outpouring of the seven bowls of God's wrath (chs.
15–16); after the victory song of Moses (ch. 15) comes the final
of the three great judgments, this one affecting the whole earth
(ch. 16—the judgment at the opening of the seals affected a
quarter and the judgment at the blowing of the trumpets a third
of the earth).

The rest of the book is divided into three great sections, with
chapters 17–18 announcing the fall of Babylon, chapters 19–20
describing the events of the day of the Lord, and chapters 21–22
describing the new heaven and the new earth. In chapter 17
Rome/Babylon is pictured as a great harlot riding on a scarlet
beast (note the similarity to the red dragon), but destined to be
destroyed by the very beast she worships (vv. 15–17). The final
fall of Babylon and the funeral dirge of the kings, merchants, and
ship captains that served her are recorded in chapter 18. Chapter 19 appropriately begins with a series of hallelujahs (the only
ones in the entire New Testament) and celebrates the wedding
supper of the Lamb and the return of the King of kings to defeat
once and for all the forces arrayed against the divine plan. This
is followed in chapter 20 by the millennial reign of Christ (with
Satan chained but then released at the end of the period) and

the final judgment of the dead. At the end all of God's opponents—the two beasts along with the dragon and all those who
stood against God—are cast into the lake of fire to suffer eternal torment. (At this point the reader must be reminded that
certain key questions—like the millennial issue in chapter 20—
cannot be answered by inductive study. The purpose of this
approach is to chart the development of the text and to get a
preliminary idea of how it all fits together.) Finally, chapters
21–22 describe the new heaven and new earth that will descend
and usher in eternity. According to chapter 21, this holy city will
be a perfect cube like the Holy of Holies, and the Shekinah presence of God with his people will characterize eternity. In 22:1–5
heaven is described as the final Eden, reinstating what the first
Eden could have become, with the tree of life now available to
the people of God. The rest of chapter 22 promises that Christ
will return soon and warns the people of God to be ready and
to remain faithful at all times.

From charting the whole book we now turn to charting the
individual paragraphs. Now we do for the small section what we
did for the whole book, that is, map out each paragraph to see
how its argument develops. Here we follow the same process we
used with the whole book, namely, we note where the thoughts
change to another issue or emphasis. We simply look for the
changes of focus as the text develops.

To continue the study of Philippians, let us work with 2:6–11,
where Paul may be quoting a hymn sung in the early church. The
primary change of emphasis occurs between verses 6–8 and
verses 9–11, which treat, respectively, Jesus' role (humility) and
God's role (exalting Jesus to glory), the two main points of the
passage. In the first main point, verse 6 stands by itself, while
verses 7–8 belong together, centering on the fact that Jesus
"made himself nothing" (a better translation than "emptied himself," v. 7) and "humbled himself" (v. 8). The rest of verses 7–8
relates the specifics of how Jesus made himself nothing and hum-

bled himself. The second main point (vv. 9–11) also has two sub-points: God's exaltation of Jesus (v. 9), and his twofold purpose for doing so, that "every knee should bow" (v. 10) and "every tongue confess" (v. 11). The key here is to note when verses are stating similar ideas (as in vv. 7–8 and vv. 10–11) and when they express separate ideas (as in v. 6 and v. 9); hence our divisions are verses 6, 7–8, 9, and 10–11. The main points and subpoints are then collated into an outline that charts the progression of ideas in the text.

This method also works well in the Old Testament, where we find main clauses primarily and very few subordinate clauses. Here a grammatical diagram is not quite as helpful as in the New Testament. Let us use Zephaniah 3:14–17 as an example. Verse 14 obviously stands apart, with three successive commands for Israel to sing and rejoice. Then in verse 15a similar divine actions are detailed: "The LORD has taken away your punishment, he has turned back your enemy." In verses 15b–16 the result is expressed, and again all the material is similar: Israel will never again fear. Finally, the Lord's presence and disposition are expressed in graphic language in verse 17: the divine warrior Yahweh, victorious over Israel's enemies, loves and rejoices in his people. This passage could yield a fourfold outline or (better in my opinion) a threefold outline combining the middle points because they supplement one another (God has turned back the enemy, so Israel need not fear anymore). The first point of the passage then is the command to God's people to rejoice (v. 14), the second point the reason for rejoicing (God has removed their punishment and they need not fear, vv. 15–16), and the third point the divine response (Yahweh the victorious warrior loves his people, v. 17).[6]

The inductive approach has two benefits. First, it produces a preliminary outline that organizes the book and its paragraphs in such a way that, when we undertake detailed deductive analysis, we will be constantly reminded of the context surrounding the passage being examined. Second, inductive analysis immerses us in a basic understanding of the passage; as a result, we will not merely copy whatever the commentaries say. It is easy to assume that scholars know so much that they must be correct in everything. However, that is not true; a cynic might argue that scholars just have more expertise in reading the text the way they want to. Our goal is to work with commentaries and other tools, not simply parrot their conclusions. An inductive study yields a preliminary understanding enabling us to work with commentaries constructively and critically rather than naively.

Deductive Study of the Text

The greatest problem in interpretation is distance or the culture gap between the world of the Bible and our world. It is difficult enough when I talk with my wife. She grew up on a farm, while I am a city boy. When we discuss things, we often discover that we are using the same words but with different meanings. How much greater is that distance when people have grown up in two different cultures, say Europe and the Orient. There is often a language barrier as well as a cultural barrier. Now multiply that by two thousand years and also keep in mind that when interpreting Scripture we are dealing with a culture that ceased to exist in A.D. 70 (when Jerusalem and the temple were destroyed, a disaster that forced Judaism to rework its religion). When I discuss things with my wife or my teaching assistant (who grew up in Korea), we are able to clarify misunderstandings. But there is no one around to clarify cultural or language issues in the Bible, so without help it becomes very difficult to understand the original meaning of Scripture.

This is why deductive study is critical—it helps us cross the gap to the ancient culture and meaning behind the Old and New Testament passages. Certainly the biblical writers intended to be understood. Paul especially kept clarifying himself to make certain no one could misinterpret what he said. Obviously, the Bible wants to be understood on its own terms. In the following material we will make the case that it *can* be understood on its own terms. This is the task of deductive analysis. By itself inductive study can do no more than clarify major emphases and structural development. It cannot yield the original intended meaning, for we will always read biblical passages in light of what the words mean today rather than what they meant to Isaiah or Paul. Scholars have studied the words in their original contexts and provide invaluable help in recovering the historical meaning.

Another benefit of deductive analysis is that a heightened understanding of the original context more often than not adds very exciting nuances to personal Bible study. I have found that wonderful devotional experiences attend the discovery of deductive insights. For instance, "Abba" (the Aramaic term for "father") in Jesus' prayers and those of the early church (note the "Abba, Father" of Mark 14:36; Rom. 8:15; Gal. 4:6) was the most intimate term for "father" in Judaism, indicating a divine Father who relates to us as his children in the most intense way.[7] This knowledge transforms our own understanding of prayer: through prayer we participate in Jesus' sonship and experience a God who loves us at the deepest possible level.

There are four basic subject areas in the exegetical ("drawing the intended meaning out of the passage") study of Scripture— literary context, grammar, word meaning, and historical-cultural backgrounds. In reality, all are examined simultaneously in deep Bible study, for they inform one another. However, each is also a separate area of consideration and so should be studied separately. As we study a passage, we should remember that our goal is to recover what God was saying to his people through the original author. Therefore, we seek the author's intended meaning in the passage. Commentaries of course cover the passage only phrase by phrase and discuss each element in isolation from the other words and phrases. This yields a false impression, for words and phrases do not carry meaning apart from the whole context. We must therefore be ever conscious of the meaning of the whole and not just of isolated parts. Every word or phrase has real meaning only as part of the whole message, so we must keep reconstructing the meaning of the entire paragraph (and then each section of the text).

1. *Literary Context.* In a sense we discussed context in the section on inductive Bible study. However, we dealt there only with the structure of the context, while here we are discussing context as a necessary ingredient in discovering the meaning of a passage. Also note that we do not have the historical context in view here (for discussion of the social and cultural background behind a passage see pp. 106–12).

The literary context is in many ways the final arbiter for all decisions regarding meaning. It has enormous influence on grammar and semantics (word meaning), our next two topics. Grammatically, for instance, the decision as to whether "love of God" means "divine love," "love from God," or "love for God" depends entirely on the context in which the phrase is found. If the larger passage is discussing God's attributes, "divine love" is the meaning. If it is discussing Christian affection for one another, "love from God" is the meaning. And if it is discussing worship, "love for God" is the meaning. Semantics is equally influenced by literary context. The truth is that very few words have meaning apart from context. If I utter "right"/"write" apart from a context, the listener has no idea which term is being used, and no idea whether it means "correct," "look to the right," or "write this down." I tell my students that if they are daydreaming and don't hear the question when I call on them, they have a 50–50 chance of being correct if they just say "context," since so many of my questions expect that as the answer.

There are many levels to the literary context. The primary force in making interpretive decisions is the immediate context, the sentences and terms surrounding the verse being studied. In some ways it could be argued that the *only* legitimating force in such decisions is the immediate context, for all words derive their meaning from the passage in which they are found. Broader spheres (like other parts of the book, other books by the author, and the rest of the Testament or the Bible) still have influence, but they provide only possible meanings and do not determine the actual meaning. For instance, the other uses of the word *joy* in Philippians do not determine its meaning in 2:2 ("make my joy complete"), although they do show how Paul tended to use the word in Philippians. In fact, its uses in the immediately preceding passage (1:25), in the immediately following passage (2:29), and in its verb form in 2:17–18 do not determine its use in 2:2. In the other passages it refers to true rejoicing, but in 2:2 it is used ironically of Paul's unhappiness with the arrogant bickering at Philippi. Often in commentaries we read arguments like, "Eleven times out of twelve in this book the word means —, so here it must also mean —." However, what if the context favors the secondary meaning, or even a third possible meaning? It is certainly true that an author's primary use of a word has great potential for the passage being studied, but we must not conclude that the primary sense is the actual meaning until it can be shown that the context favors it.

We must be even more cautious when making deductions from the rest of an author's corpus (e.g., from another epistle of Paul, or, when one is studying Luke, from Acts), or from the rest of a Testament (e.g., from the use of a word in John or 1 Peter when one is studying Paul). Each of these concentric circles has less influence the further we go from the center, but on the whole each sphere is important. On this basis the least influential sphere is genre; we have in view here parallels from extrabiblical literature of the same type as the book being studied (e.g., wisdom, apocalyptic, or legal literature in Jewish or Greco-Roman writings). However, such parallels are still important. For instance, in studying the meaning of the symbols in the Book of Revelation, it is helpful to search the whole genre, that is, to see how the terms are used in Jewish apocalyptic writings of the inter-testamental period. For a great deal of the symbolism in the Book of Revelation, for example, the locust plague or the jewels, such parallels are critical, since they tell us how Judaism used such symbols in its apocalyptic writings. Therefore, each sphere of literary context is helpful, but the final arbiter is always the immediate context.

There are two rules for interpreting on the basis of literary context.[8] First, every statement must be understood in terms of its natural meaning in the context within which it is found. What is important is the contribution of the statement to the meaning of the whole passage. None of us ever utters a sentence meant to be taken out of context or understood on its own. The same is true of Scripture. The writers were trying to get a whole message across. This is very true of the Gospels, one of the places in the Bible where passages are commonly taken out of context. Gospel episodes like the baptism or transfiguration were not meant to be seen as isolated stories, but were part of an ongoing message. In Mark, for instance, the transfiguration culminates an entire series of interwoven stories. In 6:30–8:21 Mark uses graphic terms to portray the failure of the disciples to grasp who Jesus is: hardened hearts (6:52; 8:17), blindness and deafness (8:18). Then in 8:22–26 there is an astounding two-stage miracle as Jesus heals a blind man. The miracle there also functions as a parable, for it has discipleship connotations going back to the blindness of the disciples in 8:18. Then in the ensuing sections their blind misunderstanding is also healed in two stages, first in a partial way as Peter at Caesarea Philippi understands Jesus' messiahship in blurred fashion (8:27–33; cf. 8:24) and then in completeness at the mount of transfiguration (9:2–9; cf. 8:25). In the Gospels, as elsewhere in the Bible, context is always determinative for meaning.

Second, any text apart from a context all too often becomes a pretext. This refers to the tendency to use passages out of context to prove a point without checking their true meaning. Two examples will suffice. Isaiah 1:18 ("though your sins are like scarlet, they shall be as white as snow") has often been used of spiritual salvation, while the context of verses 16–17 ("seek justice, encourage the oppressed") demonstrates that it is actually speaking of social justice, and the sins in view are committed by God's people, not pagans. In similar fashion, Revelation 3:20 ("behold, I stand at the door and knock," RSV) has also been used of the conversion of the lost, while in actuality it calls for the repentance of the Laodicean church. Unless we make sure that the passage we quote actually teaches the point we want it to make, it becomes only a pretext for our preconceived views rather than the actual Word of the Lord!

2. *Grammar.* Grammar, the relationship between words, has always been everyone's least favorite subject in junior high (high schools seem to be afraid of the subject, and I've known English majors in college that have not had a course on grammar!). In reality, grammar is the critical part of context, more so even than word meanings, for it is in the relationship between the words in a sentence that context is born. English uses word order to determine the use of the words in the sentence. In "he studies the text," the word before the verb is the subject ("he"), and the word after the verb is the object ("text"). In Greek, as in German, the inflection or ending of a noun tells how it is used in the sentence. Word order in Greek tells us what terms are being emphasized. In Greek the sentence could read "the text studies he," and "he" would still be the subject by virtue of its ending; its being placed last would give it emphasis. A similar situation occurs in John 1:1, the classic text on Jesus' divinity— "the Word was God" *(theos ēn ho logos).* The subject, "the Word" *(ho logos),* is placed last for emphasis; and in Greek a subject coming after the verb "to be" retains the article *(ho,* "the") so that the reader knows it is the subject. The lack of the article with the predicate nominative "God" *(theos)* both distinguishes

the predicate nominative from the subject ("the Word") and denotes that Jesus is "divine" (*ho theos* is normally used of God the Father). The Jehovah's Witnesses make a grammatical error in arguing that the text means "the Word was a God."

The problem with discussing grammar in basic Bible studies is that laypersons lack knowledge of the original languages Greek and Hebrew. However, this does not mean that grammar is of no use. There are two ways to overcome this problem. One is to use a literal translation like the New American Standard Bible (NASB) as a control and compare other translations with it. The NASB tends to be a literal translation of the original languages, while the New International Version (NIV) is less literal. Of course, the overly literal rendering of the NASB makes it a very clumsy translation to read, since its style is more like Greek and Hebrew than English in many places. However, it is a good study Bible for that very reason. The second way to delve into grammar is to use detailed commentaries like the Word Biblical Commentary and the New International Greek Testament Commentary. The difficulty here is their extensive interaction with the original languages. One way to overcome that problem is to memorize the Greek and Hebrew alphabets and to buy an interlinear Bible, that is, a Bible with the Greek or Hebrew side by side with the English translation (usually the English also appears directly under each Greek or Hebrew word). An interlinear will help the student identify the particular term or phrase a commentary is talking about. This latter method is for the more serious students, but can be enormously fruitful for anyone with the energy and time to use it.

A detailed discussion of Greek and Hebrew grammar is beyond the purview of this work.[9] Most of us will have to depend on the better commentaries, but there are still some basic (even fun) things that can be done. For instance, we can explore the possibilities of participles. Participles can either borrow the force of the main verb of the sentence (and thus be seen as another main clause) or can be turned into an adverbial clause (a clause beginning with a subordinating conjunction like "while," "after," "because," "so that," "in order that," "although," or "if"). It is necessary to try out each possibility to see which best fits the context. It is also a good idea to check the translations for their preference. Let's consider the participle in Philippians 2:6. The original Greek reads "being in the form of God" and modifies the following main clause, "[Christ Jesus] did not regard equality with God a thing to be grasped." In this case the NIV rather than the NASB has the literal "being in . . ."; the NASB translates, "although He existed . . ." (so also NRSV). Several other versions (JB, NEB, TEV) translate the participle as another main clause (e.g., "he always had the nature of God," TEV). Some commentaries prefer a causal "because he was by his very nature God." The reader must try each possibility to see which best fits the context. Personally, I prefer the concessive "although." Paul seems to be saying that Jesus' preexistence was divine, but in his incarnate state he did not have to seize upon recognition of that fact; a concessive "although" is a good way to express that idea.

The important thing to remember is that every grammatical option is a different translation option. It is imperative to determine which option best fits the developing argument of the text itself. It is not only the scholar who can do this. All of us can begin the great adventure of interpreting and translating the Scriptures. Of course, the option we select must be checked carefully on the basis of the criteria for testing competing interpretations (see pp. 82–83). If several commentaries reject our option, we need to interact with their arguments carefully before continuing to hold it. Also, if our decision is completely new and leads to reworking existing doctrine, we must tread very carefully and check with our pastor and other mature Christians before moving too quickly on our great insight. Every teacher has experienced some fervent Christian coming up with an "exciting new insight from the Lord" that turns out to be virtual heresy. All of us need to corroborate our new discoveries with other Christian leaders. As Paul says in 1 Corinthians 14, prophets must be judged by other mature prophets (the same is true with teachers and students of the Bible), for all of us make mistakes.

Another exciting grammatical issue that we can all interact with in the New Testament concerns genitives ("of" phrases). Whenever we find a noun modified by an "of" phrase, there are several possibilities for interpretation. Let us use Philippians 2:1 ("the fellowship of the Spirit") as an example: the genitive can be descriptive ("spiritual fellowship"), possessive ("the Spirit's fellowship"), source ("fellowship from the Spirit"), objective ("our fellowship with the Spirit"), or subjective ("the Spirit's fellowship with us"). Several versions and commentators take the "of" phrase as an objective genitive (the Philippians' "fellowship with the Spirit"), while others take it as a source genitive ("fellowship made possible by the Spirit"). In light of the parallel constructions in the verse ("encouragement in Christ" and especially "comfort of love"), it seems as though some sort of source is implied, that is, comfort is caused by love, and fellowship is caused by the Spirit. While the NIV separates these constructions ("comfort from his love," "fellowship with the Spirit"), the parallelism is close, so I see a source genitive here.

An even more important genitive is found in Romans 1:17 and 3:21—"the righteousness of God." This little phrase virtually contains within it the theme of the whole book and so is hotly debated. The same options exist. Some have argued for a possessive genitive ("God's righteousness"), others for a source genitive ("righteousness from God"), a subjective genitive ("God declaring us righteous"), or an objective genitive ("our righteous deeds before God"). The New Revised Standard is the only version that remains neutral, "righteousness of God." The NASB and NIV construe the phrase as a source genitive, while the Jerusalem Bible sees it as possessive. When we consider the context, especially the thesis paragraph of Romans (3:21–26), with its strong emphasis on justification, it seems that a combination of source and subjective genitives fits best. God has declared us righteous (the very definition of justification) in Christ.

Verbs are more difficult for one who does not know the original languages. The *Discovery Bible*, prepared by Gary Hill, tries to help the student overcome this lack of knowledge by placing signs above the verbs to indicate their force. That can be helpful. On the whole the Greek present tense is progressive in force, picturing ongoing action. The Greek aorist looks at the action as a completed whole, and the perfect tense points to a state of affairs resulting from an action. In Hebrew there are two so-called tenses, imperfect (incomplete action) and perfect (completed action). Both can occur in contexts that describe past, present, or future events. The individual context must tell the reader the force of the verb.

In both New Testament and Old Testament situations, readers will need commentaries to help them.[10] Yet studying the verb can have enormous benefits. In Romans 12:1 Paul exhorts believers to "present your bodies a living sacrifice" (KJV). Much has been made in some quarters of the fact that the verb is an aorist infinitive. On the grounds that the aorist is a once-for-all tense, it is argued that the verse teaches a second work of grace; what believers are instructed to present entails a second crisis experience subsequent to salvation. However, the aorist does not have this force. In fact, the aorist was the basic tense for infinitives in Greek, where it often tended not to have its own force, but to reflect the force of the main verb. In this context what Paul commands is to make an ongoing commitment (the main verb is present tense) of oneself to God. This interpretation also fits the verbs of verse 2 ("stop conforming . . . but keep on being transformed"), which command continuous action. Romans 12:1–2 commands a lifelong attitude of self-sacrifice and transformed spiritual living.

In summary, it is important to note closely the grammatical development of a passage. See how clauses relate to one another, and how words within the clauses relate to one another. I recommend beginning at the larger (clause) level and then proceeding to the smaller (word) level. Those without knowledge of the original languages can note how various translations and commentaries handle the text. The next step is to ask which potential grammatical translation best fits the context as a whole, and rank the options in terms of greater and lesser probability. Many, perhaps all, of the options will make sense, and so we must ask which best fits the whole. Often this will be a judgment decision, but that is the heart of interpretation. We must always be asking which option makes a greater contribution to the whole passage than do the others, and which makes better sense.

3. *Word Meaning (Semantic Research).* We have reached the heart of this chapter, the search for meaning. Yet it is critical to realize that words have no meaning apart from their grammatical relationship to the other words in the immediate context. So we could not discuss word meaning until we had considered literary context and grammar.

The science of semantics is a very recent phenomenon. It was not applied seriously to biblical studies until the last half of the twentieth century; consequently, many helpful books from the previous era like those of Richard Trench, Marvin Vincent and W. E. Vine, and Kenneth Wuest have to be used quite carefully in light of the many errors in their discussions of word meanings. One of the basic errors was the assumption that words should be studied primarily in terms of their historical development. The danger of this can be demonstrated by English words today. In some instances the meaning of a term a few centuries ago has no influence on current usage. Moisés Silva gives a couple of good examples. One could argue that ranchers should be mistrusted because originally "rancher" was linguistically related to "deranged," or that clergy should be rejected because "clergy" was linked with "calamity," or that dancing should be forbidden because "ballet" comes from the Greek word for "devil."[11] These are all exaggerated examples, but the point is that no language uses words on the basis of their ancient meaning but only on the basis of their current meaning.

Yet we constantly hear biblical words discussed in terms of past connotations. It has been said (e.g., by William Barclay, following Trench) that the word for "servant" comes from two Greek words, "to row" and "under," and that servanthood thus means accepting the lowest place, like those slaves on the lowest bank of rowers on a trireme ship. The problem is that this meaning stemmed from Homer, not from the time of the New Testament, and was probably unknown to the New Testament writers. It makes a good illustration but has nothing to do with the original intended meaning in the Bible. If the original meaning is our goal, we must be wary of injudiciously reading into biblical terms meanings that stem from a prior period.

Another common mistake, one that I still find myself making frequently, is reading several possible meanings of a word into its use in a particular passage. James Barr calls this "illegitimate totality transfer,"[12] a phrase with which we all need to become familiar. It means that we wrongly ("illegitimate") read into ("transfer") a particular text all ("totality") the meanings that the term has throughout the Bible. This is also called overexegesis, meaning that we read more into the text than is warranted by the context. For instance, whenever we study or teach a text with the word *prayer* in it, we are tempted to read all the prayer theology of the whole Bible into that verse. Barr himself notes the misreading of the term *ekklēsia* (church) in Matthew 16:18, where scholars at times have read nearly every New Testament connotation into the term. While in specific texts it can mean "assembly," "body of Christ," "community of the kingdom," or "bride of Christ," all four are not equally valid for Matthew 16:18.[13] Commentaries make this mistake frequently. When a scholar has spent days tracing a term through the intertestamental literature, Greco-Roman writings, Josephus, and the Talmud, it is difficult not to want to read a great deal of the findings into the text.

The meaning of a word depends upon two factors: the range of possible meanings it had at the time it was written, and the influence of the immediate context upon that range of possible meanings. Words are actually arbitrary symbols, that is, collections of sounds that through convention have come to signify something. There is no particular reason why "tree" means something while "qochkipf" does not, except the one came to be used in English while the other did not. The task in studying a writing is to discover why a particular word is used and what it is supposed to signify.

Walter Kaiser notes four primary aspects to meaning: reference (the concept or object denoted by the word), sense (what the usage of the term in the context of the passage is saying about that concept or object), intention (the hints in the text as to how the writer wishes to use the term), and significance (the impact upon the contemporary reader).[14] All four aspects must be considered when we are trying to determine meaning. The interplay between "the man of lawlessness" and "the restrainer" ("the one who holds back") in 2 Thessalonians 2:3–8 is a case in point. The reader must decide whether the former is the Antichrist and whether the latter is government or the Holy Spirit (or one of the dozen or so other options) and then ask which option best fits the context, how that option affects the meaning of the context as a whole, and what is the relevance for today.

From A. C. Thiselton I would add a fifth aspect of meaning. Language is meant not just to impart information but to cause action. Language by its very nature calls for response on the part of the reader, and this is especially true of biblical language. We could say that language imparts information, accomplishes an action of its own (e.g., it may suggest, request, or promise), and forces an effect upon the reader.[15] Every passage studied carries out an action and has an effect, and these are a critical part of the meaning of words. We cannot study the section on the man of lawlessness without being affected by the concepts presented, and Paul himself demands that the reader then do something: "So then, brothers, stand firm and hold to the teachings we passed on to you" (v. 15).

The student of the Word will first of all try to determine the range of possible meanings the term itself could have (called the semantic range). A person who knows the original languages can study the better lexicons, which will provide the variant possibilities.[16] A person who does not know the languages can use a combination of commentaries, Bible versions, and *Strong's Exhaustive Concordance*. For the student who knows Greek (or at least knows the alphabet and can use an interlinear New Testament) there are major linguistic tools that trace the meanings of words and provide incredibly rich resources for word study, sometimes containing as much as thirty pages on a single word.[17] The main thing is to ascertain the options for the word being studied, and then to let the immediate context filter them out until the most probable meaning remains. For instance, take the word *goal*. It can denote a purpose; a net for basketball, soccer, or hockey; a score in those sports; and the terminal point of a race. All depends on the context in which the word is used. Also, note that the word *goal* by itself does not have meaning, only meaning potential, until it is used in a context.

Examination of the context is essential in Bible study. A basic error is to assume a word always has the same meaning and to read that meaning into the biblical text wherever the word appears. For instance, most assume that "sanctification" or "holiness" always refers to the process of spiritual growth subsequent to salvation. However, in Romans 6:19 and 1 Corinthians 1:2 the term refers to the moment of justification itself. Also, in James 1:2–4, 12, *peirasmos* (trial) means a crisis situation or problem that arises. However, the verb form of this term is used in 1:13–15 to speak of the "temptation" that is presented by the trial. We cannot assume that a word always means the same thing. The context has to tell us.

Let us look at a problematic passage. In Philippians 2:7 Paul says that Christ "emptied himself" *(ekenōsen)*. Many throughout history assumed that the verb means that Christ emptied himself of his divinity (cf. v. 6), and thus there developed the so-called kenotic school considered by most to be heretical. Scholars continued to wrestle with the problem for centuries. Recently, however, it has been realized that a semantic approach provides the answer. The primary meaning of the verb is indeed "to empty," but it can also mean "to destroy," "to make of no effect," or "to deprive," and as an intransitive (i.e., a verb without a direct object) it can mean to "make oneself nothing" (NIV) or "take the lowest place." This latter meaning is certainly the thrust here, making the verb virtually synonymous with "humbled himself" in verse 8. This rendering of the verb solves a centuries-old problem and also has the advantage of fitting the context much better than do other interpretations (like "emptied himself of his privileges but not of his deity," which always remained a clumsy explanation).

Another problem in word studies centers upon synonyms. It is quite common to read more into the use of different terms than is warranted. The classic example is John 21:15–17. There Jesus asks Peter, "Do you truly love *(agapan)* me more than these?" and Peter responds, "Yes, Lord, I love *(philein)* you." In the past, it has been common to assume that this involves two levels of love, divine love *(agapan)* and human affection *(philein)*. However, recent studies have shown that in John both terms are used of the Father's love for the Son, both of the Son's love for the Father, both of the love of Father and Son for the believer, both of the believer's love for the Father and the Son, and both of the love of believers for each other. In other words, they are synonymous. In fact, in the short passage of 21:15–17 there are two words for "love," two words for "know," two words for "tend," and two words for "sheep." John is using synonyms to develop his main point, that love for Christ involves pastoral responsibility to tend the flock of God.

The proper way to study synonyms in the same context is to let the passage itself determine whether the terms have the same meaning or are different nuances of the concept. For instance, in Philippians 4:6 there are four terms for prayer, "in everything by prayer and supplication with thanksgiving let your requests be made known to God" (NRSV). It is very likely that the three terms "prayer," "supplication," and "requests" are synonymous, with "thanksgiving" the perspective within which prayer is offered. From the context it would be difficult to make the case for different types of prayer. However, in Hebrews 10:8, "sacrifices and offerings, burnt offerings and sin offerings you did not desire," the terms sum up the various types of sacrifices in the Old Testament system. Each use of synonyms in the same context is a separate issue and must be decided on its own merits.

Let us now develop a method for doing proper word study.[18] We will use Zephaniah 3:14–17 (NASB) as a test case (see p. 89). First, in studying the passage, determine the key words in the context. Gordon Fee suggests four ways of doing this: note terms that are theologically loaded ("daughter of Zion" in v. 14; "King of Israel" and "LORD" in v. 15); note critical terms that at first glance seem ambiguous ("be quiet" in v. 17); note repeated terms or concepts that become themes ("exult" in vv. 14, 17; "do not be afraid" in vv. 15–16); and note terms more important in the context than appears at first glance ("victorious warrior" in v. 17).[19]

Second, study carefully the context in which the terms occur. Zephaniah 3:14–17 occurs in a prophecy of judgment promising the day of the Lord (1:7–2:3) against the nations (2:4–15) and Judah itself (3:1–5). Yet God's mercy would be experienced by the righteous remnant in terms of inheriting the land (2:7, 9) and worshiping their God (3:9–13). The book concludes on the note of Yahweh's deliverance of and love for his faithful remnant.

Third, study each term in light of its semantic range and use in its immediate context. "Daughter of Zion" builds upon the development of the term *Zion* in the prophetic period as the sacred name for Jerusalem, the city of God's coming salvation. Each key noun in verse 14 ("daughter of Zion," "Israel," "daughter of Jerusalem") is used in the book only of the righteous remnant ("Israel" also in 2:9 and 3:13; the others only here), and so their joy is based not upon the historical situation, but upon their realization of who they are before God. This conclusion is furthered by the titles of God chosen here. "Yahweh" is the covenant name of God as the ever-faithful Lord who never leaves nor forsakes his people. "King of Israel" tells them that the Lord, not any apostate king on the actual throne of Judah, is their true King who watches over them. So the command not to fear is based not upon their situation, but upon the Lord who watches over them. Their confidence abounds in him. Moreover, the command to "exult" in verse 14 is clearly based upon the God who "exults" in them (v. 17). It is a two-way street. Finally, this God is a "victorious warrior" who fights his people's battles for them and then quiets them in his love. The term *gibbōr* is translated "mighty to save" in the NIV, but is used of a "warrior" in 1:14, so it is likely that Yahweh is seen in 3:17 as a divine warrior (a constant image in the Old Testament) who fights the battles for his people and delivers them. This divine warrior first of all wins the battle for his faithful followers and then returns to quiet their fears. There is hardly a more powerful picture of divine love in the Bible than in verse 17!

4. *Historical-Cultural Backgrounds.* We have already studied the literary context of the biblical text. Now we must consider the historical context behind the text. The problem of the historical gap or distance between the biblical period and our own is

solved by studying the historical-cultural background behind the passage. "Historical" here refers to the ancient situation within which the biblical author wrote his work, and "cultural" refers to the manners and customs alluded to within his work. The importance of studying this background cannot be overstated. Consider, for instance, the case of the Book of Zephaniah, written in the seventh century B.C. just before the reform of Josiah (621 B.C.). The prophet warned Judah to repent and abolish the pagan practices instituted during the evil reign of Manasseh. In the prophecy God threatens Judah with being overrun if they do not repent. This knowledge enables the reader to bridge the gap between that time and ours and to enter the thought world behind the book. The details of the book can then be studied in light of the situation it addressed.

A difficulty for us today is that the background information for individual texts was often presupposed by the original author. When the ancient writers produced their works, they sometimes explained the customs alluded to in the text (e.g., Mark 7:3–4 explains for Gentile readers the Jewish religious custom of washing the hands before a meal), but more often than not they did not do so. The reason is that they shared basic assumptions with their readers, who understood the customs and did not need to have them explained. Living in a radically different culture, we have to be informed about ancient practices if we are to understand the text completely. A similar situation exists today. Sitting in on a conversation between people from Los Angeles or New York or Chicago can be a difficult experience. They keep alluding to things we might know nothing about, and to make sense of the conversation we must keep asking them to clarify details. Of course, this does not mean that the biblical text cannot be understood at all without knowledge of background details. Rather, it means that one dimension (a very enlightening and exciting dimension) will be missing. Our purpose here is to explain how to recover historical details.

The major problem in uncovering background material is the paucity of the evidence. Edwin Yamauchi has shown how fragmentary the evidence is, since so few archeological sites have been excavated, and of the material excavated so little has actually been published.[20] However, he recognizes that quite a bit of knowledge has been uncovered, and we can be fairly certain of background details supported by, for example, written traditions, inscriptions, and pottery. In other words, it does not take a massive amount of evidence to establish the existence of a custom. In fact, the explosion of knowledge in this area over the last few decades has been staggering.

The letter to the church at Laodicea (Rev. 3:14–22) provides an interesting example. Commentators used to interpret "I wish you were either [hot or cold]" (v. 15) in terms of spiritually hot or cold. However, Colin Hemer sums up recent research showing that the reference is actually to Laodicea's water supply.[21] A few miles to the north was Hierapolis with its famed hot springs, and a few miles to the southeast was Colosse with its cold pure drinking water. The people of Laodicea, however, had no natural water supply. They had to pipe their water in via aqueducts, and when it arrived, it was lukewarm and filled with minerals. To drink it was to vomit (hence "I am about to spit you out of my mouth," v. 16). The Lord is saying that the Laodiceans, for all their wealth and power (they were famed for their banking, black wool, and medical skill; see vv. 17–18), resembled their water. They made God sick! The background material adds great power to the text. In fact, Hemer shows that this is characteristic of all seven letters in Revelation 2–3; each letter addresses the situation of the individual church and the city in which it was located.

There are several areas from which background data can be drawn.[22] Geography is important in most of the historical or narrative material of the Bible. In fact, any study of Joshua or Judges is incomplete without geographical knowledge. Barry Beitzel shows that the conquest of Canaan followed almost the same contours as the Six-Day War of 1967; geography in both cases dictated the military operations.[23] The study of politics helps us to understand Israel as a buffer between Assyria and Babylon and between Persia and Greece. In fact, Israel has often been called the most fought over piece of real estate in history because it was the land bridge between Eurasia and Africa. Many of the problems described in the latter books of the Old Testament reflect this fact. Economics helps to explain the situation of the poor in both Testaments as well as many of the pressures upon Israel. For instance, when David conquered the Syrians and captured a thousand chariots (2 Sam. 8:3–4), he hamstrung most of the chariot horses because he did not have the means or technology to use them. Later Solomon was able to use chariots (1 Kings 10:26) because he had improved the economic situation of Israel. In addition, a knowledge of ancient military tactics explains several difficult passages. For instance, Abraham with only 318 men defeated a large force (four kings) because he chose to fight in the canyons of Mount Hermon near Damascus, where a small force had a military advantage (Gen. 14:14–16).

Cultural practices should also be considered. Family and education customs provide many insights. Parents were responsible for most of the education of their children. After being weaned, sons were taught religion and a profession by their father. Gifted or wealthy children might go to a school, but that was rare. Manhood was assumed at puberty.[24] This makes all the more astounding Jesus' remarkable knowledge of the Torah at age twelve (Luke 2:46–47).

Material customs touching on home and dress are also informative. Most homes had flatbed roofs made of wooden beams with hard-packed dirt (at times grass grew on them, Ps. 129:6); wealthier homes had Hellenistic tile roofs (Luke 5:19). These roofs served as dining rooms and places of entertainment. In

New Testament times men often wore both an undergarment called a tunic (a linen piece reaching from the shoulders to the knees) and an overgarment called a cloak (a heavier piece reaching close to the ankles). When in sending out the Twelve Jesus forbade them to take a second tunic (Matt. 10:9–10; Mark 6:8–9), he was referring to an extra piece taken on trips for warmth while sleeping. His general instructions (no money, no bag, no extra tunic) center on the need to depend on God rather than self when one is engaged in mission. Similarly, knowledge of athletics and recreation can illuminate such passages as Isaiah 40:30–31. The "young men [who] stumble and fall" were the great athletes of their day, all of whom were military men. The "brave warriors" of Israel were famed for their swiftness (1 Chron. 12:8). In 1 Corinthians 9:24–27 Paul combines imagery from the sports of running and boxing.

Of course, uncovering such details can be difficult. However, commentaries, encyclopedias, and dictionaries provide valuable aid. Here as much as in any other area the student will be dependent on secondary sources. There are a growing number of very fine sources just on background information.[25] The table of contents and the indexes of these volumes will point the student to whatever should be known.

The danger in such historical study is that the event can take precedence over the text, that is, we can spend so much time reconstructing what originally happened that the text is left behind. Then we end up with revisionist history: the text is actually rewritten and ultimately falsified with an imaginative reconstruction. This is exemplified in Norman Gottwald's massive *Tribes of Yahweh*, in which he rewrites the conquest of Canaan as a Marxist-type internal revolution of a peasant class in Canaan, the Hebrews, rather than an invasion by tribes from outside Canaan.[26]

Most of us are in no danger of doing such a thing, but it is easy to overdo backgrounds. Let me note Luke 16:1–9, the parable of the unjust steward or shrewd manager, as an example. This passage is difficult because in verse 8 the master (literally, "lord") seems to applaud an act of dishonesty: having been fired for wasting the master's money (vv. 1–2), the shrewd manager makes friends for himself by altering the accounts of his master's debtors (vv. 5–7). For several years I was enamored of explanations utilizing background information to make sense of the parable, namely that the altering of debts was not an act of dishonesty but removal of either the exorbitant interest being charged[27] or the manager's commission.[28] However, I slowly began to realize that the text of the parable gives no hint of such background, and that these theories may read far too much into the story. In reality, this parable is one of the best examples of a phenomenon in Jesus' parables called "reversal of expectation": Jesus twists the story by introducing actions that would never happen in real life, like the master's commending the steward's shrewdness when the steward has just cheated him. Jesus uses this incomprehensible twist of plot to force us to think about his spiritual point at a deeper level. Here Jesus' point has to do with a "shrewd" use of our money to make friends for ourselves via almsgiving (vv. 8b–9).

The key is to remember that we cannot use background information unless the text itself points to it. That is, the text itself will give us some indication when such information will prove helpful. If we encounter some detail, such as the debate between the Pharisees and Sadducees over the resurrection from the dead (Acts 23) or the pieces of armor in Ephesians 6, and realize the text doesn't explain it to us, then it is time to trace the historical background. Such knowledge is part of the intended meaning of the text, since the author presupposed that the readers knew it; it will be helpful, then, for us to understand it as well. With regard to Ephesians 6, it adds a great deal to realize that Paul was writing while imprisoned in Rome. He would have been wearing a light chain on his wrist attaching him loosely to one of the very Roman infantrymen whose armor he was describing! The belt was a broad sash of cloth, about six inches wide, that held the armor tight to the body and provided back support in the midst of battle. The footwear was a sandal-like piece of supple leather with lacings up the calf and with studs on the sole to allow the soldier to march more steadily over difficult terrain and to hold the ground more firmly in the midst of battle. The shield was the Roman great shield, about five by three feet in size, that was used to protect soldiers from the fiery arrows shot at a high arc against infantrymen. The sword was the greatest military development in the ancient world; made of superior metal, it was razor-sharp on both sides and came to a sharp point at the tip. It was so invincible that the Roman army was called "the short swords."

Let me suggest some criteria for using background material properly. First, it is a supplement to exegetical study and not an end in itself. It cannot replace word studies but is in a sense another type of word study, arising out of the context behind and suggested by the language of the text. Second, when commentaries disagree about the background (as in the case of Luke 16), the larger context must decide which account fits the text best. Any option that fails to make the meaning of the text clear is less likely than the others. Third, if extrabiblical literary material is suggested as a parallel, ask whether it actually fits the passage being studied. Some of this material may fit a scholar's pet theory more than the passage itself. Be aware of this danger. Do the context and language of the alleged parallel actually cohere with the context and language of the biblical passage? Always remember that the biblical material has precedence; it is primary, not the potential background information. Finally, seek parallels between the background situation, once you have determined that the author actually does presuppose it, and your own situation.

Applied Study of the Text

The value of studying historical background is that it makes the passage come alive. The drama of the text in its original context adds an excitement to serious Bible study, for we can almost breathe the air and feel the tension of the original situation and message. This then makes it easier to face similar situations in our own lives.

The true goal of Bible study is not the learned essay or the original meaning of the text, but the implications of the text for our daily lives. God never intended for his inspired Word to be merely an object of research but a guidebook for life. We are to act upon it, not just learn it or come to understand it. In Hebrew the word *hear* in another stem means to "obey." In other words, we have not "heard" until we "obey." Note Joshua 1:8, "Do not let this Book of the Law depart from your mouth; meditate on it day and night, *so that you may be careful to do everything written in it.* Then you will be prosperous and successful" (italics added).

Until recently there were no works on principles for hermeneutical application. All one could find were pragmatic discussions dealing with the how-to of application; there were good illustrations, for example. It was the missiologists who began to explore this dimension of Bible study under the rubric of contextualization, which refers to the cross-cultural communication of biblical truth. The implications for application are obvious. The same principles for properly communicating the Bible to an overseas culture pertain to the communication of the Bible to our own culture. The quintessential cross-communication is, of course, from the ancient cultures of biblical times to the many cultures of our own time, whether African, Asian, European, or American. In every case we seek the relevance of the first-century truths of Scripture for twentieth-century needs. The teaching about eating meat offered to idols (1 Cor. 8–10) is more directly applicable in the idolatrous cultures of Asia and Africa and less so in our own (our idols are money and success), but in every culture we seek to relive the Bible's timeless truths.

The danger comes with failure to appreciate the need to maintain the truth content of the Bible and also to address contemporary situations. Extremes on both sides of the equation abound. Sometimes the explication of Scripture is so content-oriented as to downplay or even reject application. Some so-called expository preachers refuse to apply at all and just teach the objective meaning of the text, expecting the hearers some-how to recognize immediately what they are to do about the passage. This rarely works well, for application can come only with serious reflection on the implications of the text for today. On the other hand, some ignore the meaning of the text and apply the passage directly without considering what the author intended to say. This can lead to syncretism, in which the cultural situation has precedence over the text.

The key in contextualization and application is to recognize the distinction between content and form. The content (meaning) of biblical truth is unchanging, while the form in which it is presented to the life of the church changes with the situation. Contextualization is dependent on the demands of the biblical text, not vice versa. To fail to recognize this is to sink into relativism. Should we, then, negate the fatherhood of God in a matriarchal culture or in response to demands from radical feminists? (In Oxford University Press's new Inclusive Language Version, the Lord's Prayer begins, "Our Father-Mother who is in heaven. . . .") Should we surrender the biblical teaching that homosexuality is a sin because that teaching is not politically correct to modern intelligentsia? The key is to allow the dynamic between the text and the modern situation to work itself out. The text establishes the agenda, and we seek to relive its message in practical situations.

Figure 3 visualizes the process of contextualization. We must first discover "what the text meant," that is, its original intended meaning; then we must determine "what the text means," that is, apply it to our own lives. These two elements are inter-dependent. We should not focus on one without the other.

Figure 3
The Process of Contextualization

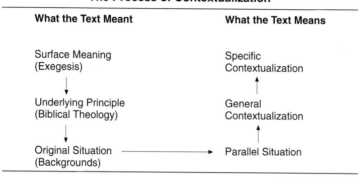

What the Text Meant	What the Text Means
Surface Meaning (Exegesis)	Specific Contextualization
Underlying Principle (Biblical Theology)	General Contextualization
Original Situation (Backgrounds)	Parallel Situation

In the first stage, working with the original surface meaning of the biblical text, we find that the author did not intend merely to impart cognitive information, but to apply or contextualize those truths to the lives of his readers. In other words, contextualization already occurs in Scripture itself. As we study or exegete the text, we are already seeing application occurring. Paul is applying deep truths of the gospel to the situation of his readers. For instance, in the hymn of Philippians 2:6–11, which we have already studied, Paul is using the theology of incarnation to establish Jesus as a paradigm or model for believers. He is not just telling who Jesus is; rather, Jesus' model of servanthood challenges the Philippian leaders to exemplify humility (2:3b–4) rather than self-serving arrogance (2:3a).

The second stage studies the deeper theological principles behind the author's surface message. (The tools for discovering the biblical theology behind a passage will be discussed in ch. 3.) The task is to study the larger idea behind the one presented in the text. As the author wrestled with the problems in the church to which he was writing, he decided to utilize certain theological truths in addressing that specific situation. In other words, the text we are studying is already contextualizing a broader theological truth to solve an issue in the church. For instance, two terms that get at the heart of Peter's message to northern Asia Minor are "aliens" and "strangers" (1 Peter 1:1, 17; 2:11). The surface meaning reflects that area's status as alienated and separate from the rest of the world. The deeper theological background beneath the surface, however, stems from teaching in the early church on "citizenship in heaven" (see, e.g., Phil. 3:20; Eph. 2:19; Heb. 12:22). In other words, Peter is reminding those readers who are discouraged by persecution that this world is not their home. They are aliens and "tourists" (the meaning of "strangers") here; their true home is heaven, so they should not allow the problems of this life to overwhelm them. In the same epistle, "trials" refers specifically to persecution (1:6–7), but there and in James 1:2–4 the larger theological principle behind the teaching is the enduring of trials in general. Persecution is a specific type of trial. Peter emphasizes one aspect of the larger theological teaching in order to address the specific problem of his readers. As we study the Bible, it is very helpful to note both the surface message and the deeper theological teaching behind it. This material can be used for a deeper understanding of the passage (which is very helpful when teaching a Bible study or preaching on the passage) and as a step to good application.

The third stage studies the original situation in the church that led to the points being made in the text. Most of the time (especially in the Epistles and the Prophets) this is quite clear, and introductions in commentaries typically will discuss the situation that led to the emphases in the book. However, in historical books and in some of the prophets (e.g., Jonah and Obadiah) the original situation of the readers is hard to determine. In narrative literature we often focus more on the situation in the narrative (e.g., behind the parable of the prodigal son in Luke 15 lies the Pharisees' grumbling about Jesus' association with sinners) than on the *Sitz im Leben* (situation in the life) of the original readers.

With stage four we move to application. The importance of determining the original situation now comes to the fore, as we seek parallel situations in our life (and in the needs of our church). If we are to apply the Word of God properly, we must ask what issues in our lives the author would address if he were speaking directly to us. In other words, what issues today parallel the issues behind the teaching of the text itself? There is little value in spending a great deal of time studying the meaning of the text and then applying it shallowly to whatever we wish. While the Word of God needs to be understood correctly, even more must it be obeyed correctly, and that means in accordance with the thrust of the text itself. It would be wrong to use the "aliens and strangers" of 1 Peter to justify the type of personality that alienates others (as I have actually heard the phrase used); it refers only to relations with the secular world and focuses primarily on the arena of trials and persecution.

Finally, the last two stages pertain to the way we apply the text. We can decide to apply its message to a situation exactly paralleling that in the text (e.g., persecution in 1 Peter) or more generally to any situation addressed by the theological truth embedded in the text (e.g., trials in general). In the latter instance, we must be careful that we are in fact applying the point behind the text. Two types of passages can be applied on the general level: those with "extended application" (as in the case of "unequally yoked" in 2 Cor. 6:14 [KJV], referring primarily to close pagan friends but also applicable to marriage with unbelievers) and those with "particulars that are not comparable" (as in the case of meat offered to idols [1 Cor. 8–10]).[29] As we study the Bible and teach or preach it, we must be careful to allow it to address our lives and equally careful to make certain we allow it to do so in accordance with its divinely inspired intention. My approach is to ask at every point, how would Peter (or Isaiah or Paul) say this if he were here today? What issues would he address in my life and the lives of the people in my church?

Good Bible study is bridge building, connecting the ancient culture (and meaning) of the text with our own contemporary scene. As we move back and forth from the points of the text to the needs of our own time, we are constructing the girders and spans that tie the inspired Word to our expiring world. So deep Bible study is a continuing bridging process that helps us re-experience the power, drama, and message of the text anew. The bridge is built point by point as we move through the text, combining exegesis (the search for meaning) and contextualization (the application of that meaning to our lives).

There are three levels at which we can combine exegesis and contextualization. The process can be (1) personal and devotional (the first-person approach; see p. 78), or it can be used for (2) group Bible study or (3) a sermon (the second-person approach). In actuality, it must be a devotional experience before it can be communicated to others. Also, even devotional experiences are biblically meant to be shared. Contrary to popular understanding, there is no evidence in Scripture that the Christian life was ever meant to be lived only at a purely personal level. Every New Testament (as well as Old Testament) command is intended to be lived out corporately, that is, in the fellowship of the believers. Because American culture has developed from the frontier spirit of individualism (called "rugged American individualism"), we have assumed that biblical commands are for each of us by ourselves. This is one of the most unbiblical preunderstandings of them all! In fact, I would go so far as to call it "anti-Christian." Scripture tells us we need to help each other; we cannot live the Christian life by ourselves. Thus Hebrews 12:12, in a context centering on the struggles of the Christian life (vv. 4–11), tells us, "Therefore, strengthen your feeble arms and weak knees." This means that the strong Christians are to help the weak in times of crisis. Verse 13 goes on to say, "'Make level paths for your feet,' so that the lame may not be disabled, but rather healed." Because all of us from time to time are lame or spiritually crippled (see Heb. 5:11–6:3), we must depend on each other. Thus in studying the Bible, we should ask first how this applies to our own lives and second how we can share these wonderful truths with those around us, our family and friends. There is no greater joy than leading a Bible study or teaching a Sunday school class. I can honestly say that the greatest joy in ministry is the privilege of preaching God's Word. Preachers do not just lead worship; they worship God in their sermon and give the congregation the opportunity to join them in worship. Everyone who teaches or preaches the deep truths of Scripture is closest to God at that moment and feels the presence of the Spirit in a new and wonderful way! It is not a duty to teach or preach; it is a sacred privilege!

Contrary to many contemporary theories, modern persons cannot automatically apply the Word of God to their daily lives. This misapprehension is one contributing factor to the growing number of Sunday Christians, people who live the Christian life when in church but who out in the real world cannot (and often are unwilling to) put the principles into practice. We need to help them understand the what, the why, and the how of the relevance of Scripture for their lives. There are three major ways of accomplishing this objective as we teach or preach the Word: direct application, in which we elucidate the lessons of the text and exhort the congregation about its relevance for them; indirect application, in which we suggest ways in which the audience can participate in the process of application (here we might use pointed illustrations or stories); and persuasion and motivation, convincing the audience of the importance of the message and prompting them to act on it.

Most of us today are masters of rationalization, explaining away the reasons why we cannot live according to biblical principles. We need to have such delusions exposed and to be helped to do something about them. This does not come easily. We enjoy our pet sins, somehow feeling that God understands and overlooks these unimportant little indulgences. However, while God loves us, he hates sin, so we need help in coming to grips with those areas of our lives that are a barrier not only between ourselves and God, but also between ourselves and true happiness! This is the task of good, probing application. It can be readily accomplished when it is tied to the significance of the biblical text. The key is a wise choice of emotive language that has its origin in the text and its implications for our lives. The Bible presents direct, dramatic exhortation and encourages us to do the same. Also, we must be specific about the text's implications, helping each person to see how it affects one's daily life. Teach and preach for Monday to Saturday, not just for Sunday. Always encourage those in the audience (and yourself!) to ask, "What can I do about this tomorrow? How can I live differently at work and at home as a result of studying this text?" A mature Bible study and church are exemplified by people who come with a desire to grow in Christ and to discover areas in their lives where they can change.

A Summary of Basic Method

The reader will be excused for feeling somewhat overwhelmed by the material in this chapter. It seems far too much for a practical and personal Bible study. Let me clarify what I am asking the reader to do. The purpose of this chapter is to provide a method and a perspective for deep Bible study, not to demand more than the average layperson can do. All of the steps in the process (outlining, grammatical analysis, word study, background research, application) are meant to be done simultaneously (not as lengthy separate steps) as we study the biblical text. I am not demanding hours and hours of research into a passage, possible only for the scholar who is paid to take the massive amounts of time necessary to do all this. Rather, what I am proposing is possible for those who have a half hour or so at a time for serious

Bible study. To illustrate basic Bible study, I will reprise the principal steps and apply them to a specific passage. Building upon the earlier work on the Book of Philippians, I will be using Philippians 3:7–11 as my model passage.

Throughout this summary keep in view that there are several levels at which Bible study is done. The simplest is personal Bible study, and that is the true goal of this chapter. Someone who is leading a Bible study will take more time and do a more detailed analysis of the text in order to lead others into it. A pastor wil' take still more time (ten to twenty hours on a passage) in order not only to discern the meaning of the passage and its application to the congregation, but to craft the message itself. Then there is the scholar writing a major article or a commentary on the passage. Obviously, this is the most detailed of all and demands hour upon hour of primary research (into the biblical and extrabiblical parallels for the passage) as well as massive interaction with all the secondary material (articles, commentaries, etc.) written on the passage. In this concluding summary, I will concentrate on the first two levels (personal Bible study and preparation for leading a Bible study), for that is what most of the readers will be doing. At the same time, I will briefly note what could be done at the more detailed levels.

Step 1. Working with Presuppositions

As we read through the text, we should try to bring to the surface and identify our own theological presuppositions regarding the issues that the text presents. This can be done in conjunction with inductive study (step 2). As we work through the text on our own, we must be aware of our own worldview and the theological ideas we have developed. The key is to be careful not to allow our presuppositions to descend into prejudice. Prejudiced theology tends to manipulate the text to our own ends, and then we do not seek truth but conformity, that is, we have already decided what the text has to mean, and our study forces it to conform or to confirm that our views are correct. Are we willing to allow the text to challenge and even to change those views if need be? This does not mean that we cannot be comfortable with our theology. It means that we are open to rethink our views if the Bible so dictates. The goal is to work with our presuppositions rather than be dominated by prejudices. For some people their personal theology has more influence on their belief system than does Scripture itself.

The answer is an openness to truth and to the message of the text. We work with our beliefs: in one sense we bracket our theological views and allow the text to address them, while in another sense we study the text through the lens of our theological system. At this beginning stage we bring our views to the surface and are aware of them as a system of thinking, with the priority going to the biblical text. This openness to new possibilities is worked out through the Bible study itself; through our word studies and deeper analysis, we allow the text to confirm or to challenge our previously held views as the situation dictates.

Step 2. Inductive Bible Study

In studying any passage, we must be aware of its place in the larger context. Philippians 3 begins a new section, Paul's attack on the Judaizing heresy that has just come into Philippi. He addresses this serious problem in 3:1–4:1. Verses 7–11 follow Paul's opening arguments on the evil of his opponents (vv. 1–3) and on his religious pedigree, that is, his right to speak on the issues (vv. 4–6). He then presents his own attitude and perspective on what is important in life. As we look at the thought development or outline of verses 7–11, we see that the focus changes at verse 8b, verse 10, and verse 11, with a minor change at verse 8. Therefore, there are four main sections—Paul's desire to consider everything loss (vv. 7–8a), with verse 7 discussing past loss and verse 8a present loss; Paul's desire to gain Christ and be found in him (vv. 8b–9); Paul's desire to know Christ (v. 10); and Paul's desire to attain the final resurrection (v. 11). Of course, this is preliminary in the sense that further study might dictate a slightly different outline, for instance, verses 10–11 might be one point rather than two. The value of this inductive analysis is that it gives us an idea as to the thrust of the passage, and so we will not be quite so controlled by the commentaries. We will interact with them rather than accept their interpretations automatically. For a personal Bible study, a quick read-through of the passage is sufficient. For the leader of a Bible study, inductive analysis should not take more than one half-hour session. Leave many of the details for the deeper analysis.

Step 3. Deductive Bible Study

Deductive Bible study is the area where the outlay of time will vary the most. Personal Bible study will normally take one or two half-hour sessions, while a Bible-study leader may take three to five hours, and a pastor seven to ten hours. A scholar will often take several days to study a passage in depth. Yet each level will follow the same basic pattern, looking at each message unit separately and utilizing all the tools together—grammar, semantics, background, and biblical theological parallels.

Grammatically, the first unit (v. 7a), "whatever was to my profit," looks back to verses 4–6 and refers to Paul's pedigree and former success. The second unit (v. 7b), "I counted as loss for the sake of Christ" (RSV; the NIV's "now" is not in most versions or in the original), is probably written from the perspective of the time of Paul's conversion (note the past tense). The terms "profit" and "loss" reflect the language of commerce; in the spiritual accounting sheet all past success or profit was regarded as loss so that Paul could gain Christ. Verse 8 moves from past to present and applies the principle to present successes, "I consider everything a loss." (The phrase "what is more" is very emphatic.) While some think verse 8 continues from the perspective of the time of Paul's conversion, I think the switch to present tense moves the focus to Paul's present situation. This means that even his ministry successes (think of all Paul had experienced, e.g., the three missionary journeys) must be counted loss if they get between Paul and the Lord. This hardly means that Paul never rejoiced in all that he did for Christ. Rather, it is a perspective on life. What mattered to Paul was not what he accomplished but rather his walk with the Lord—"the surpassing greatness of knowing Christ Jesus my Lord." Doing things for Christ was great indeed, but "knowing Christ" had "surpassing greatness." So Paul is talking priorities.

The second major point (vv. 8b–9) reinforces the "gain-loss" antithesis and makes it even stronger by switching from nouns to verbs—"I have lost . . . that I may gain."[30] Note the intensification also in "I have lost . . . consider them rubbish." Paul's successes are not just "loss" but "rubbish," a term that can mean not only "garbage" but also "dung." There is hardly a stronger term, for it denotes something that is not only worthless but degrading as well. Paul's goal was twofold, to "gain Christ" and to "be found in him." The latter clarifies the former as a reference to the results of salvation, the new status (to "be found") in Christ. Note in verse 9 the double contrast between the righteousness "of my own . . . from the law" and the righteousness "through faith in Christ," further defined as "from God . . . by faith." The radical opposition between legal righteousness ("from the law") and divine salvation ("from God . . . by faith") is Paul's response to the Judaizers' religion "of the flesh" (v. 2c). The only way to be right before God is to cease trying to earn salvation and to simply believe in Christ.

Paul proceeds to further define his purpose as to "know Christ." Most believe that "knowing Christ" in this context goes beyond intellectual comprehension (though it includes that) to speak of experiencing Christ in our lives. This is especially true in verse 10, where Paul elaborates on the "knowing" of verse 8 with three objects—"Christ," "the power of his resurrection," and "the fellowship of sharing in his sufferings" ("sharing in" is the NIV's interpretive addition). The grammatical question is whether all three are separate objects of "to know" or whether the latter two are aspects of "knowing Christ." Whichever we decide (I tentatively prefer the latter), knowing Christ means also to experience his resurrection power, a concept seen also in Romans 4:25 ("raised to life for our justification") and 6:4 ("just as Christ was raised from the dead . . . we too may live a new life"). To know "the power of his resurrection" is to "walk in newness of life" (Rom. 6:4 NASB) or to live a life of spiritual victory. Yet it also means to share in his "sufferings," a concept paralleled in Colossians 1:24 ("I fill up in my flesh what is still lacking in regard to Christ's afflictions") and Romans 8:17 ("if indeed we share in his sufferings in order that we may also share in his glory"). The sacrifices and trials of the believer are not experienced in isolation, but are part of sharing in the life of Christ. This is the deepest kind of fellowship with him. The means by which it is experienced is to unite not just with his life ("the power of his resurrection"), but also with his death (I would translate "by becoming like him in his death"). This thought also goes back to Romans 6 (v. 5, "If we have been united with him in his death, we will certainly also be united with him in his resurrection"). For Paul the supreme paradox of Christianity is that death is the path to life, which reverses the human experience. For us to live in Christ, we must die with him to self, sin, and the things of this world.

Finally, verse 11 tells us the ultimate goal: "to attain to the resurrection from the dead." Paul throughout his writings centers upon our participation in Jesus' resurrection (note 1 Cor. 15 in addition to the passages in Rom. 6 and 8 that we cited above). For Paul the resurrection is the culmination of everything; without it all Christian preaching and belief are "useless" (1 Cor. 15:14). The big question in Philippians 3:11 is whether "and so, somehow, to attain" (literally, "if somehow I might attain") means that Paul saw a danger of apostasy. There is a tentativeness to this statement, but whether one sees the possibility of apostasy here (in contrast to the confidence of security in passages like Rom. 8:17, 30–31, and 1 Cor. 15:51–58) will somewhat depend upon whether one's preunderstanding is Calvinist or Arminian. This passage could be interpreted either way.

Step 4. Applied Bible Study

Finally, we ask how the passage impacts our lives and the lives of those around us in the church. This is accomplished by seeking contemporary situations that parallel those of the Philippian Christians. There are two situations in the text: the problem of Judaizing heretics and their influence on the Philippians, and the general situation of Christian life and experience that Paul is using to address the problem. Parallels today would certainly be the inroads the cults are making in our churches and the need to anchor Christians in a deep Christian walk to counter that pressure. Thus this passage applies directly to us today. Verses 7–8 relate to the need we all have to negate ("consider loss") those past and present successes we count upon to feel good about our Christian walk. Ministry for Christ is detrimental when it leads us to replace our worship with our work. This is a problem that every Christian leader faces. Jesus wants us more than he needs our accomplishments. So we like Paul must count all our status and plaudits as "rubbish" and seek to know him, not just to do things for him. Verse 9 anchors this principle by speaking of our very experience of justification. We did not earn our salvation on the basis of our goodness or our religious accomplishments. We simply believed in Christ and received salvation as a free gift. Therefore (v. 10) we are to live our Christian life not just on the basis of what we do but whom we know, namely Christ. In the final analysis, it is not by our own power and talents but by his resurrection power that we can be successful. It is not by our own sacrifices but by consciously reliving his sufferings that life becomes meaningful. Finally, our true goal should not be success in a worldly sense (and this includes building big churches and writing great Christian literature!), but resurrection from the dead in a heavenly sense.

Recommended Reading

William W. Klein, Craig L. Blomberg, and Robert L. Hubbard, Jr. *Introduction to Biblical Interpretation.* Dallas: Word, 1993. A very good mid-level discussion of most issues related to interpretation of Scripture. Bible students will find this volume very helpful and easy to understand.

Grant R. Osborne. *The Hermeneutical Spiral: A Comprehensive Introduction to Biblical Interpretation.* Downers Grove, Ill.: InterVarsity, 1991. A comprehensive introduction to the field, including discussions of theology and homiletics. The language at times can be daunting and the discussions complex, but serious students will find most issues treated.

Robert H. Stein. *Playing by the Rules: A Basic Guide to Interpreting the Bible.* Grand Rapids: Baker, 1994. The best lay-level introduction yet produced. It is very readable with interesting metaphors for the aspects of serious Bible study. It is the simplest of the three, yet has something for everyone.

Can We Get Theology
from the Bible?

e was one of the brightest grads the seminary had produced. He was gifted, energetic, a wonderful communicator, and extremely likable. He had it all. He had planted a church in a small town, and it had flourished—over two hundred members in less than two years. Then he started a series of messages on 1 Corinthians 12–14 without knowing where his people stood and without preparing them theologically for the difficult issue of spiritual gifts. In one of the messages he mentioned that he believed the supernatural gifts were still available for today, and the wealthy woman who gave much of the money that ran the church exploded. She believed not only that the gifts had ceased, but that on that basis his position was heresy. Within six months the church had ceased to exist, and he left a defeated man. Today he still has not returned to the ministry.

This sad scenario has occurred all too often, and it is certain to occur time and time again in the future. Two factors contribute: we do not really know how to determine dogma, especially how to get it from Scripture, and we have no idea how to distinguish cardinal doctrines from those on which we should agree to disagree. There are more heresy hunters running around than at any time in recent memory, and yet there is less theological awareness in most churches than at any time this century. It is a strange dichotomy—more material on the Bible and theology than ever, more interest in Bible studies, and yet less knowledge of the Bible and theology. There is much work to be done, and it is my hope that this chapter will contribute to the solution.

It must be stressed that churches do not really have less interest in the Bible and theology. As I minister around the country and especially overseas, I see people who want to be fed, who enjoy expository preaching and have a desire to learn more about God's truth. The problem lies with the leaders more than with the laity. A currently popular philosophy of ministry says that members of the television generation have short attention spans and need to be entertained with interesting stories rather than be taught biblical truth. Therefore the content of the average sermon has gone down rather markedly in the last couple of decades. But this is not because people are not interested in good theological preaching and teaching. It is because they have not been trained to recognize good theological preaching and teaching. Two things contribute to this: the seminaries are not doing a good enough job of training their students to make theology interesting and oriented to life, with the result that leaders don't do much with theology in their ministries; and people have not learned to distinguish between quasi-theological moralizing and true theology. I have seen instances in which church members have heard deep biblical preaching one Sunday and said, "That's just what we need!" Then the next Sunday they heard a message with funny stories and limited depth and again responded, "That's just what we need!" Often people want to be fed but do not quite know what that entails. Yet it is clear that the disjunction between biblical content and engaging illustrations is a false one. The Bible is a fascinating book, not a boring one, and expository messages that unfold biblical texts can be very stimulating. The same is true of theological preaching. I am arguing here that we need to preach and teach theology in our churches, and these studies will be well received. Thus the thesis of this chapter is "back to theology!"

In essence theology is reflection on God and his relationship to this world, especially to the people of God. Building upon the Bible, theology has been created by centuries of serious thought on the meaning of Scripture for life and faith. However, as David Wells has so cogently said, "Theology is a knowledge that belongs first and foremost to the people of God and . . . the proper and primary audience for theology is therefore the Church, not the learned guild."[1] This is precisely the problem today. It is the academy, not the church, that is taking over theological reflection. Theology is no longer being used to edify the saints, but is more and more the province of learned debate. When it does appear in the church, it does not nurture so much as divide the congregation. Internecine wars develop rather than spiritual growth, and judgmentalism replaces meditation.

This does not have to be so. It is my hope that this chapter might help stem the tide and return theology to the heart of the church. In the Bible the purpose of "sound doctrine" (1 Tim. 1:10; 6:3) is clear. It provides "teaching, rebuking, correcting and training in righteousness" (2 Tim. 3:16). It is the basis for our hope (Titus 1:9) and our growth in Christ (Col. 2:6–7). As such it must be passed on to reliable people who, guarding and defending the faith "once for all entrusted to the saints" (Jude 3; cf. 2 Tim. 4:3), will in turn teach the next generation of believers (2 Tim. 2:2). In the early church, theology was a precious heritage that directed Christians in their walk, guided their relationships with the world around them, informed their worship, and protected them from false teaching. It should fill the same purposes today.

Where Is Theology Today?

Richard Muller tells the story of a new "doctor of ministry" graduate with many years of practical experience. Speaking at graduation as the representative of his class, he thanked the seminary for finally developing a relevant program. He told how he had never been particularly pro-seminary, but had worked toward the doctorate of ministry because it was a practical, how-to degree "that demanded no theological speculation, no academic, ivory-tower critical thinking, no retreat from the nitty-gritty reality of daily ministry"; he had wanted "only useful, relevant subjects."[2] Needless to say, the faculty winced often during that talk! At Trinity Evangelical Divinity School a couple of years ago, a student whose senior sermon was critiqued as having good style but poor content replied, "You don't understand. I've been preaching in a little church for the past couple of years, and my people are just not interested in the Bible or theology. They want to know how to live their lives in a practical, day-by-day way." This perception is quite common, and its roots need to be traced.

Charles Swindoll in his *Growing Deep in the Christian Life* discusses the problem of theology in the local church. He points out that theology is the victim of a "bum rap" and consequently ranks far behind issues like family life and self-help in terms of perceived value. The average Christian does not realize how critical theology is and understands far too little about it. The reason is twofold. First, lay people "have convinced themselves that (a) they don't need to fuss around with heady stuff like that since they aren't doing 'full-time ministry,' or (b) even if they made a study of the doctrines, all that knowledge would be of little practical value."[3] Second, the theologians have not made theology understandable. Their language is above the head of the average person, and their explanations are too lengthy and complex to make sense. "As a result," says Swindoll to the theologians, "much of what you write is kept within those cloistered chambers that intimidate people who haven't had the privilege of probing the heavenlies as you have. The majority feel a distance from you when you share your secrets."[4] Swindoll argues that both laypersons and theologians are at fault. To the former he points out that all Christians are full-time ministers, and all aspects of biblical and theological knowledge are practical for life. Also, theology does not have to be so complex that it cannot be understood.

Two other recent works have studied the causes of this theological malaise, David Wells's *No Place for Truth, or, Whatever Happened to Evangelical Theology?* and Os Guinness and John Seel's *No God but God: Breaking with the Idols of Our Age.* Before I build upon their conclusions, however, I must state one caveat. In such prophetic works (and in a lesser sense, my own discussion to follow), there is inevitable hyperbole. The negative critique that follows does not indict the whole evangelical movement, for there are pockets of real concern for theological matters. Let me note one letter in *Christian Century* in response to an article by John Cobb stating that churches have forsaken theology and relegated it to the professionals at the academy:

> In my corner of the church there are very lively discussions going on among clergy and laity. . . . Pericope groups, clergy support groups and informal meetings in the hallways at churchwide gatherings are often filled with "cutting edge" theological discussions. . . . I would feel more comfortable if theological teachers like Cobb would spend their sabbaticals as a pastor in a local parish before they spout off and say that theological reflection is marginalized out here.[5]

The letter makes a good point. There is theological reflection occurring in many churches, and laity want to be taught. The problem is that (with some exceptions) they are all too often not being taught. Again, I feel that the problem lies not with the laity so much as with the leaders. Also, the interest in theology is more with the highly controversial issues than with theology as a whole. There is very little systematic theology going on, that is, very little desire to construct a theological model that links doctrinal issues together into a systematic whole. One rarely hears a sermon series on the doctrine of God or the doctrine of the church. I agree with Guinness and Seel, who see the problem in a broader sense as a need for revival and reformation in the church. Accordingly, their book begins:

> It is time once again to hammer theses on the door of the church. As on the occasion of Martin Luther's ninety-five theses in the sixteenth century and Søren Kierkegaard's single thesis in the nineteenth century, Christendom is becoming a betrayal of the Christian faith of the New Testament. To pretend otherwise is either to be blind or to appear to be making a fool of God.[6]

These are strong words, but most would agree with their general tenor. The evangelical movement is in trouble. Statistics cited by Wells indicate that over 70 percent of the public believe they are evangelicals, while only about 16 percent understand what the gospel is all about; moreover, the statistics on divorce, teen pregnancies, and general immorality in the church are frightening. In other words, never in the history of our nation has the evangelical church been more popular, and never has it made less of an impact on societal mores.

In fact, just the reverse has happened. The church instead of countering has been captured by the ways of the world. In the language of Romans 12:2, we have been "conformed to this world" (RSV) or, in the striking paraphrase of the Phillips version, been "squeeze[d] . . . into its own mold." The central thesis of both Wells and Guinness-Seel is that the church has capitulated to the lure of modernity. Wells speaks of "the process of social change that has resulted in our urban-centered life" (modernization) and of our consequent acceptance of "values that seem, despite their relativity and anti-religious bias, to offer the only appropriate ways of looking at life amid the technological pyramids that we are building" (modernity).[7]

In and of themselves, of course, technology and the scientific wonders of our age are not bad. The problem is that we have accepted the inventions and the system that produced them wholesale and uncritically. Not only the materials but also the values of our age have crept into the lives of Christians. With the rugged individualism that we have inherited from the frontier past, private religion has more and more replaced public concerns.[8] Other factors in this development are that the urban environment, with its mass culture, is inherently impersonal, and the high mobility of our society has eroded the sense of community. People attend church, but all too often have few if any close friends there, so fellowship becomes a rare commodity. As a result, more and more people situate spiritual authority in themselves rather than in the church, and this makes it easy for rationalization and secularism to rule the day. Secularism is the value system behind modernity, and as Wells points out, we are now living in the first society in history to consciously try to define itself without any religious assumptions or recognition of the divine.[9] This influence is seen in Christian circles as well, primarily in the secularity with which we conduct ourselves. Private experience has replaced theological awareness, and doctrine has given way to emphasis on "felt needs." Consequently, theology, when it does appear, is used more to settle disputes than to direct lives.

To demonstrate this problem further, let us consider Guinness's critique of church growth.[10] The church growth movement, which, in view of the success of the megachurches, may be the most influential religious phenomenon of the 1990s, has lofty, commendable goals such as mission, church renewal, growth, and relevance. However, one must question whether relevance has been taken too far, for several problems have surfaced: (1) "Church" is taken to mean the local church rather than the universal church; as a result, an unfortunate competition for numbers has arisen among local churches, to the detriment of the gospel. (2) "Growth" is seen more in quantitative than in qualitative terms, and the goal of making disciples has been replaced with a shallow evangelism (remember that the Great Commission enjoins the discipling of all nations, not just evangelism). (3) There are very few biblical controls; modern methods are utilized without asking whether they might conflict with Scripture. "Theology is rarely more than marginal . . . and discussion of the traditional marks of the church is virtually non-existent. Instead, methodology, or technique, is at the center and in control. The result is a methodology only occasionally in search of a theology."[11] (4) There is little awareness of history or interest in its lessons, which could protect the movement from critical errors. (5) The process of contextualization and the quest for relevance have not been biblically controlled, but have descended to compromise with and capitulation to secular techniques. Being seeker-friendly and market-driven is viable only when it does not go too far, that is, when it leads to true conversion and spiritual growth rather than to a new kind of shallow group therapy. (6) The social sciences are used and assumed to be true without question "by church leaders who forget theology in the charge after the latest insights from sociology—regardless of where the ideas come from or where they lead to."[12] (7) There can be a practical atheism when the techniques of modernity are uncritically utilized and replace divine truth; God is ultimately left out of the picture, and this is idolatry.

The solution is to make God and his truths central in all Christian endeavors, to be culturally relevant without being culture-bound. This can occur only when every technique and method is subjected to the searching critique of biblical and theological truth. Let me give one example. The homogeneity principle of the church growth movement states that churches should seg-ment society along economic and ethnic lines and reach each group independently. The problem is that this runs counter to the emphasis upon ethnic unity in Ephesians and economic unity in James. Subjecting the principle to biblical and theological truth tells us that homogeneity is valid for evangelism (reach people where they are) but not for church growth. Paul reached Gentiles as Gentiles and Jews as Jews ("all things to all men," 1 Cor. 9:22), but then demanded that they form one church.

Another cause-symptom of theological malaise is that the phi-losophy of ministry has changed drastically in the last couple of decades. Christian leaders are seen more and more as managers and psychologists rather than truth brokers. Wells states that as a result of the privatization of religion, "the responsibility of seeking to be Christian in the modern world is then transformed into a search for . . . a 'technology of practice,' for techniques with which to expand the Church and master the self that bor-row mainly from business management and psychology."[13] Fill-ing practical needs has become more important than theologi-cal truth, and professionalism than godliness. Ministry has become more market-driven than Scripture-driven, and the practical needs of being successful and making a difference have been given greater place than have serving God and communi-cating his Word. This is illustrated in Leadership magazine, a major professional journal. Wells categorizes its articles from 1980 to 1988: 80 percent concern personal and professional crises among the clergy; 13 percent discuss techniques for managing the church; less than 1 percent of the material makes any clear reference to Scripture.[14] I remember the issue on expository preaching; there was little reference to Scripture, and all the arti-cles were on preaching to various psychological needs in the con-gregation. Also, note the changes in the primary lay magazine, Christianity Today, between 1959 and 1989: advertising went from 3–7 to 30–48 percent of the available space; religious news went from 20 to 40 percent; book reviews from 15 to 9 percent (with a corresponding move from mostly academic books to mostly semipopular Christian literature); biblical and doctrinal content declined from 36 to 8 percent.[15]

Wells further notes that the roles of the clergy have shifted.[16] According to one study, the top three requirements of a minister are planning ability, facility in leading worship, and sensitivity to the congregation. Duties of somewhat lesser importance include spiritual nourishment, counseling, visiting the sick, and leading in stewardship; finally come administering the church, getting the laity involved, and supporting worldwide mission. Two aspects dominate—technical or professional competence and psychological nourishing. None of the duties relate to the communication and preservation of sound doctrine (à la Paul)!

There is an element of hyperbole in what has been said. The problems are real but not insurmountable. The difficulty is widespread but not universal. As I go from church to church, there is interest in biblical and theological truth, and many leaders are feeding their flock. An article by Richard Mouw has turned the critique of Wells and Guinness on its head, arguing, "When theologians dismiss as 'tacky' the religious experience, thought, and longings of the untutored, they risk missing their main target: serving God's people. . . . Why are so many theologians inclined simply to denounce these phenomena rather than to work to establish them on more solid theological foundations?"[17] Mouw believes that popular religion should be seen as an important starting point for theological reflection; thus theologians should affirm the vitality of popular religion and deepen its understanding. Lay people can add the element of everyday life to theology, a dynamic that is as needed in the philosophical musings of the professionals as their theological depth is needed by the laity. Mouw makes a good point. It is indeed too easy simply to critique the popular movements and to overstate the extent of their influence. We need balance, and we need to work together.

However, there are a few areas where Mouw himself has missed the point. First, it is not so much the laity as the leaders who are developing the popular movements, and they should know better. In some instances there is indeed not merely ignorance of, but rejection of theology in favor of method. Second, method tends to replace theology, not just implement it. Most of the techniques, if placed under the watchful eye of biblical and theological controls, would be helpful indeed, but only if their excesses could be so checked. Third, I agree that there is nothing inherently dangerous with managerial, sociological, and psychological insights. However, it is not psychology but psychobabble that the critics find dangerous. It is not sociology but a market-driven misuse of statistics that is so sadly mistaken. Wells and Guinness are not criticizing balanced, biblically based methodology. Christian psychologists themselves disown the pseudopsychology too often in control today.

Our aim here has been simply to document the crisis in theology. Though not universal, it is increasingly a problem. Theology is essential and critical because it enables layperson and leader alike to understand the relationship of God and his Word to the needs and problems of our day. We in the academy and the pulpit must learn to make it exciting and practical as well. Techniques and methods should supplement, not replace, theology at the center of a philosophy of ministry.

Influences on Our Theology

Every one of us has a theology. It may not be developed, but we all have a view of God, an opinion as to how he relates to us, and an idea as to how we should relate to him and to each other. Yet where do we get such views, and how can we decide which are valid and which are not? There are four components of theological formulation, four elements that together form the basis of the ideas we have about God, our world, and our place in it.

Logically, their order of importance is Scripture, tradition, community, and experience. Scripture should provide the basis for everything we believe, and the ecclesial tradition within which we grew up should help us make sense of and organize our belief system. However, in terms of actual influence upon us, the order is virtually reversed, so we will discuss in turn experience, community, tradition, and Scripture.

1. Experience

"Experience" refers both to the events that have shaped our lives and to the worldview or belief system that has resulted. We approach life on the basis of the experiences we have had, and they have formative influence on the way we interpret the world around us. These life situations have a major influence on our view of God and play a determinative role in the way we develop our religious language and thus our beliefs.

It used to be said that the theologian needs to be objective, that is, to stand outside belief systems and to make rational decisions regarding religious truth. However, as Wentzel Van Huyssteen says, "The way the theologian, as a Christian believer, experiences his or her faith and the nature of religious language are mutually determinant of the status of theological statements, both in theology itself and in philosophy of science."[18] In other words, scholar and layperson alike look at the world around them and God's place in that world on the basis of their experiences. All of us shape our lives and interpret reality through eyes that are the composite result of what we have gone through. It is in vogue today among many nonevangelicals to believe that this context or life situation is the critical factor in shaping modern theology. In their search for a theology for our time they argue that religious beliefs should not be based on past experiences (for instance, those from the Bible), but should reshape those past examples to meet current needs. In other words, biblical truths are not normative; rather, they provide models that must be reapplied to contemporary needs in order to develop a relevant theology for today.

Evangelicals oppose such blatant attempts to rewrite Scripture and theology, because these efforts produce a culture-bound Christianity that ceases to be Christian at all. However, evangelicals must also ask whether some popular forms of Christian teaching and preaching really differ from this radical approach. It is the current fad to base preaching and teaching upon the "felt needs" of the audience and to stress psychological well-being over the whole gospel. Christian teaching is now being encased in a veneer of contemporary relevance more than in the truths of the Bible. All too often, context or experience determines the form of evangelical communication just as much as it does liberal theology.

The key is to find balance. Experience is an important aspect of our lives, and God wants to use it positively in guiding us to his truth. We can avoid the pitfalls of an overly zealous dependence on modern context by interpreting our experience via community, tradition, and especially Scripture, the other three components in theological decision-making.

2. Community

Our church community has tremendous influence upon what we think and believe, for the teaching that occurs there is a primary religious input in our lives. Few of us fall back merely upon our personal experiences to interpret the reality behind our world or to provide us our worldview. That interpretation usually comes from the faith community of which we are a part. Of course, this does not mean we naively accept everything we are told. However, our questions are asked and, for the most part, answered in the context of our church and its teachers. In other words, we are theologically the product of that community. When we disagree with certain views in our church, we usually dialogue with others on those issues. Sometimes we agree to disagree; at other times we continue to challenge those around us. Most of the time, however, we forge our theological views in our church context.

The community's beliefs must be grounded in the past, in tradition and Scripture, not just in the teaching of the moment. I remember hearing someone say that a gifted speaker with a terrific personality could virtually lead the average evangelical church into heresy in five years without losing more than 25 percent of its people. That certainly may be exaggerated, but all too many place charisma over content. Community is an important factor in our theological thinking, but it must not become the final factor. It must be controlled by tradition and especially by Scripture.

3. Tradition

"Tradition" refers to the historical development of a religious group's set of beliefs and practices. Most evangelicals are somewhat unaware of their traditions, and many in fact have rejected any such notion. Overreacting to the centrality of tradition within Roman Catholicism,[19] several low-church movements have rejected creeds and dogma and live under the mistaken view that there is no tradition behind their theology. Nothing could be further from the truth. Pastors of independent and of fundamentalist churches are at all times part of an ongoing historical movement and have accepted certain tenets of that movement. Those tenets are part of their tradition, and they can become all the more binding when people are unaware of their source. When we say that we follow Scripture, we must be cognizant of the fact that we interpret that Scripture, and that what we are following may actually be but a set of beliefs we have long accepted. When we say that the Bible makes a particular affirmation, that affirmation all too often may be merely what our tradition maintains. We must not, without checking our presuppositions, naively believe that the Bible is the source.

This is not to say that the tradition we inherit is the enemy of truth. Our theological tradition provides data and an essential framework for understanding the Bible, and we all need system for our beliefs. In fact, that is the subject of this chapter. It is an exciting adventure to both trace the roots of the various aspects of our religious beliefs and to discover the interrelationships between them. The key is to remain aware that what we are dealing with is tradition, and to use it positively in the search for biblical and systematic truth.

I have been on a couple of commissions examining how biblically and denominationally orthodox the views of certain theological groups are. In several of these groups one common factor stands out. Their founders sought to derive doctrine straight from Scripture without recourse to any other system of theology. At first glance that seems admirable. They wanted the Bible, not other people's views, to determine their beliefs. However, this approach is very dangerous. First, it presumes that we can study the Bible inductively by ourselves and discover the objective truth in it without input from any other system or tradition. None of us can do so, for we are all the product of our experiences and community, and thus bring certain presuppositions with us. In every case I examined, the leaders, without realizing what they were doing, read Scripture in light of their preconceived ideas. The guidelines suggested in chapter 2 (pp. 121–22) for dealing with our presuppositions apply here as well. Second, tradition provides a set of controls upon extreme ideas and helps us to realize when we have gone too far in our interpretation. When well-meaning leaders reject all tradition, they also lose all control, and most of the time the result is an aberrant theology.

It is important to realize that at its heart tradition is interpretive. Each creed and dogma developed within a concrete historical situation in the life of the church and applied the broader teaching of Scripture to that situation. It is critical that the church today continue to work with the theological deposit inherited from the past and both reexamine its biblical sufficiency and restate it for the contemporary church.

4. Scripture

We would like to believe that Scripture is the formative factor in determining our theology. We presuppose that dogma develops automatically from biblical texts. We read or memorize a verse, and doctrine emerges almost unbidden. What we do not realize is that our theological understanding all too often is controlled by the three components already discussed. These three—tradition, community, experience—form the triumvirate of our preunderstanding. As we approach biblical texts and try to collate them theologically, we cannot help organizing them on the basis of our preconceived approach to religious truth as derived from these three components.

At the core of the issue is our view of biblical authority. If the Bible is the inspired, inerrant Word of God, it will provide the content and testing ground for all doctrinal claims. But we frequently take our own interpretation as the authentic message of the text and never examine whether our interpretation is valid. In fact, we often assume our interpretation is not only the meaning of the text, but the text itself. This leads to a pearl-stringing approach to dogma: we string favorite passages together to prove a doctrine. We never notice that our opponents do the same, stringing together their favorite passages to prove an entirely different doctrine. In other words, the proof texts of the two sides are mutually contradictory, and neither side notices! They do not really listen to each other but instead spend their time preaching to the converted in a triumphalistic sort of way. What we need is to obey our view of scriptural authority by examining all the texts on both sides and then developing a balanced doctrine that fits all the biblical data. This means that, if necessary, we will have to abandon our previous position and allow the texts to determine our final doctrinal statement.

Those who do theology from a liberal perspective cannot accept the ultimate authority of Scripture for theological formulation. For instance, Gordon Kaufman states that the Bible liberates one from all bondage, even that of religious traditions. Also, the Bible itself is the product of a traditionalizing process within the life of Israel and the early church, so it cannot be binding. As a result, theology itself undergoes constant reformulation as the historical context changes.[20] Paul Achtemeier states that inspiration is seen not only in the original events behind the Bible and their codification in Scripture, but also in the canonical process and in the later interpretations of Scripture by succeeding church communities, including our own.[21] For these scholars the Bible witnesses to the presence of God in the world and provides models for Christian thinking, but is not normative or binding for contemporary theology.

For the evangelical, of course, the Bible is the Word of God and must be obeyed as the final and only source of religious truth. Liberals point to the plurality of competing theologies and ask if we can ever actually claim to attain a definitive set of doctrinal truths. It is certainly correct that evangelicals differ widely in their systems and their approach to truth. However, there is also universal acceptance of what may be called the cardinal doctrines of the faith, such as the Trinity, the deity of Christ, substitutionary atonement, the return of Christ, and many others. Within the whole of systematic theology there is disagreement, but on the essential doctrines there is agreement, so it is untrue to charge the evangelical camp with rampant pluralism. All submit to the final authority of Scripture and work with the information and interpretations available in church traditions. The reader's preunderstanding must remain heuristic in nature, that is, open to dialogue and change on the basis of the scriptural data themselves as well as challenges from competing schools of thought. In fact, it is our very openness to these competing systems that allows us to move ever closer to the theological truths of Scripture, for these ideas challenge us and drive us back to the Word, thus making us more open to its teaching, more willing to be corrected by it. Thereby, we can find truth.

Steps in Theological Formulation

Theology results from the collation of the truths of individual texts into covering models that explicate what the Bible has to say on specific issues. On the basis of their historical development these models are then logically organized into larger sets of doctrines that communicate how God relates to his creation, to the world of humankind, and to his people. The organizing patterns are supplied by the philosophical thinking of the contemporary scene, resulting in a system that ties together all theological issues into a coherent whole. There are, then, five aspects in the development of a systematic theology—exegesis, biblical theology, historical theology, contextualization along philosophical lines, and the resultant systematic theology.

The key is to realize that inspiration resides in the biblical text; and so the biblical text, not historical theology or philosophical theology, is the final arbiter in all theological debates. Scripture provides the material, and the other components (tradition, community, experience) help us to redescribe or contextualize that material for today. The theologian's task is to interpret, collate, and reorganize scriptural teaching so that the church today can understand it and apply it to life. In this sense, the steps in theological formulation are heuristic, that is, open to further reflection and revision. They are always human approximations that seek to put together and make sense of the often disparate statements of Scripture on particular issues. The danger of systems is that within particular communities they can attain the status of virtual inerrancy, and thus the communities' belief structure becomes embedded in tradition more than the Bible. We too easily forget that our systemic models are descriptive metaphors that seek to redescribe and re-present the biblical data as a holistic teaching, to organize and structure related theological ideas.[22] As in science, theology seeks to provide a map of a whole theory, and also as in science that map or model is being continuously revised with further reflection and accumulation of data. Models attain permanent status when they become the basis of credal and catechetical expression in a worship community. Yet even then equally evangelical (i.e., dedicated to biblical truth) communities have other ideas, and so permanent status does not mean final status. Through interaction between communities and continued reexamination of the biblical basis for our beliefs, we can spiral upward closer and closer to theological truth. We trust our traditions and the systematic theology that results from them, yet we are open to further modification as we continue to reflect upon Scripture and consider challenges from other faith communities.

1. Exegesis and Theology

Exegesis refers to drawing out of a text what it means. It includes inductive and deductive approaches, in particular, structural study (how the text develops), grammar or syntax (how the words relate to each other), semantics (what the words mean in their contexts), and historical-cultural research (which ancient events and situations constitute the background to the passage). The goal of exegesis is to determine the original meaning of the entire message unit (the passage as a whole), that is, what the author wanted to communicate to the original readers. Interpreters place themselves in the shoes of the author and readers and seek to re-create what God inspired in the original context.

Systematic theology begins with exegesis, for theology in essence is a collective discipline putting together what Scripture as a whole has to say on a subject, and that synthesis starts with the exegesis of the individual texts that are collated to form the doctrine. Exegesis and theology are interdependent, each building on the other. On the one hand, theology works with the results of exegesis. On the other hand, theology provides the categories that enable us to make sense out of the individual passages. Theology is "regulative of exegesis" in the sense that the message of the Bible is controlled by "the historical framework of the revelation process itself" even more than by "literal relationships."[23]

In fact, there is a circularity in the relationship between exegesis and theology, as the two continue to interact and refine one another. Exegesis provides the data, systematic theology the synthesis of those data into covering models of biblical truth. Of course, this relationship is informed by both biblical and historical theology, as we will soon see. There is no one-way movement from biblical text to modern system but rather a complex circularity in which we interpret the texts from the standpoint of a preconceived theology and yet try to use our understandings of the text to inform and refine that selfsame theology.

For instance, when we are trying to make sense of the doctrines of security and the need for perseverance, we begin by exegeting the passages teaching security (John 6:35–44; 10:27–29; Rom. 8:31–39; Eph. 1:13–14) and the passages enjoining perseverance (Heb. 6:4–6; 10:26–31; Col. 1:23; 2 Peter 2:20). These sets of passages seem to contradict each other, so we tend to interpret them on the basis of our pre-understanding (i.e., whether we are Calvinist or Arminian). However, we also try to learn from those who disagree with us, and we continue to be driven back to the text in order to let it speak. Through biblical and historical theology we remain cognizant of the larger issues, willing at all times to let the text rather than just our theology have the final say. We are at all times aware of the historical debates on security, which keep us immersed in the text and not just in our theology. In this way we can fine-tune and if necessary change our theological position on the basis of an informed study of the biblical text.

Yet exegesis of individual texts can be given too much theological force. We must be aware that no passage contains within itself the whole of doctrine. What this means is that we cannot prove dogma merely by quoting or studying individual passages. We cannot prove our view of security by studying either John 6 or Hebrews 6. Each passage stresses one aspect of the larger doctrinal whole. We uncover dogma only by studying all the passages that apply. This is the task of biblical theology. The task of exegesis is to study each of the passages in turn and supply the data for biblical theology to put together.

In short, exegesis and theology cannot exist without one another. Biblical theology provides the framework of salvation-history, systematic theology the network of relationships between the aspects of divine truth, and exegesis the specific data necessary to the task of coming to understand the fulness of the Word of God. Without exegesis theology becomes a contentless accumulation of proof texts without proof. Without theology exegesis has no set of controls regarding meaning and theological significance and rapidly descends into subjective interpretations. Exegesis provides the data, theology both the biblical (biblical theology) and theological (systematic theology) categories that give meaning to the data.

2. Biblical Theology

There are three different ways to do biblical theology. Some (e.g., George E. Ladd, D. A. Carson) argue that the only proper approach is descriptive, analyzing the teaching of individual books or authors. To go further, for instance, to collate the data into theologies of the Old or New Testament or of the Bible as a whole, is to enter the province of systematics and to confuse the issues. Others believe that biblical theology is broader and should collate the diverse material into a theology of Israel (Old Testament theology) and a theology of the early church (New Testament theology). The key for this second approach is to restrict the study to the historical question of how the theologies of the two peoples of God developed in their respective periods. One major desire of many who take this approach is to discover the central unifying theme (or themes) tying together the biblical material. Still others prefer to take the third, that is, the thematic approach, tracing key theological issues through the two Testaments. Thus there are major works on covenant, promise, hope, kingdom, and many other themes. Here, too, some are seeking the unifying theme that unites the Testaments and the Bible as a whole.

The first two types of biblical theology are primarily done by specialists. These somewhat technical studies help us to understand the theory and issues behind biblical theology and thus to fit it into the general theological task more easily. Also, they give us confidence regarding our own ability to handle the issues of biblical theology. The third approach, thematic studies, is at the heart of the church's interest and needs and so will be our primary focus. Every serious church or study group has to work through important and controversial issues like the return of Christ (subjects of debate here include the rapture and the nature of the millennium), baptism, spiritual (charismatic) gifts, and the like. The only proper approach is to study the development of the doctrine in Scripture (biblical theology) and then to study the theology of the group (historical and systematic theology) in light of the findings. Those passages that relate to the issue will be collected, exegetically studied, and compared to decide exactly how the doctrine developed and what it meant to Israel and the early church. Yet the process is more complex.

Biblical theology finds its proper place as a bridge between exegesis and systematic theology. Charles Scobie notes three stages in the history of this discipline:

1. *An integrated biblical theology.* In the first sixteen hundred years of the church age, the church made no distinction between biblical theology and systematic theology; even Martin Luther and John Calvin considered their dogmatic theology to be biblical theology.
2. *An independent biblical theology.* From Johann Gabler and Georg Bauer in the eighteenth century to William Wrede and Krister Stendahl in the twentieth century, critical scholars have rigidly separated the two disciplines, considering biblical theology a study of religious history and thus virtually part of historical theology.
3. *An intermediate biblical theology.* Scobie argues for a new approach, situating biblical theology between the historical-literary study of Scripture (exegesis) and the dogmatic use of Scripture and biblical theology by the church (systematic theology).[24] In the world of scholarship, this is a new paradigm. Within evangelicalism it has been the view for decades.

Given this view of biblical theology as a bridge, the classic distinction proposed by Krister Stendahl of biblical theology as descriptive and systematic theology as normative makes some sense.[25] On the one hand, the distinction is problematic in that biblical theology ceases to be theological and becomes historical, part of history-of-religions research. On the other hand, biblical theology does provide a descriptive, historical synthesis of the theologies of individual texts, while systematic theology turns this descriptive framework into normative dogma. As Elmer Martens says, biblical theology is "that approach to Scripture which attempts to see biblical material holistically and to describe this wholeness or synthesis in biblical categories . . . to embrace the Bible and to arrive at an intelligible coherence of the whole despite the great diversity of the parts."[26]

Biblical theology utilizes the results of the exegesis of individual passages and begins to collate or synthesize the developing theology as it arises from the ongoing exegetical investigation. There are two ways this can be done. Technically, the "bottom-up" approach (in which topics arise as texts are studied and then are organized into longitudinal or linking themes that draw the texts together theologically) is superior, but this can be done only by the professional. (In the "top-down" approach, the categories of systematic theology are forced on the biblical books and authors.) One would develop the theologies first of individual books (Genesis, Matthew, Romans) and then of individual authors (the author of the Pentateuch, John, Paul). Obviously this would take a great amount of time, for in essence the entire Bible would have to be studied in depth. This has never been done, and many believe it cannot be done. Certain shortcuts have to be taken to avoid a fifty-year project! Mainly, the scholar makes a close reading (rather than a major exegetical study) of the individual texts, begins to collate the themes at that level, and then exegetes only the necessary portions. Such theological studies of individual books have been made and proven quite fruitful.

Next, the scholar traces the themes as they link other books by the same author (John or Paul) and organizes those themes as they emerge from the whole corpus. A recent article organizes John's theology on the basis of Christology (Word/Logos, God, I Am, Son of God, Messiah, Son of man, prophet), signs and faith, salvation (eternal life, salvation as revelation, the death of Jesus), the community and the Paraclete.[27] This is a good example of the methodology of biblical theology, for the themes (from most important to less important) emerge from the text.

A key issue at this point is unity and diversity. There is diversity in the theology of individual authors, but a larger unity in the theology of Israel and of the early church, and in the theology of the Bible as a whole. In discovering the larger unity, we must study the interplay of ideas from one passage to another. We begin with the individual texts, noticing the theological ideas that link successive passages in the biblical book. Then we note how the themes progress within the corpus of the biblical writer and finally how the ideas bridge from one author to another. In the whole process we are trying to ascertain the development of theological meaning from one expression to the next, looking for the theological threads that link together the individual statements, sections, books, authors, and finally Testaments.

The means by which we discover unifying themes and parallel passages is called "intertextuality," a reference to the interplay and development of themes that link one text with another. Parallel passages are discovered through similar wording (the same terms or phrases may be used), similar contexts (parallel issues may be discussed), or similar themes (the same issue may be discussed from different perspectives). The student studies the parallel passages to see the extent to which their themes relate to each other. From this a map or model is created that puts together all the ideas that the author has expressed on a particular issue. This amounts to his theological teaching on the issue. If the writer has produced several works, the intertextual study will expand, usually on the basis of the order in which he wrote his works or the canonical order. Next, a similar study is done for each of the other writers, and again intertextual parallels (language, context, themes) unlock each author's theology. Now comes the difficult task of comparing the diverse theologies of the authors and discerning those points at which their theologies intersect. Those points become the longitudinal themes that bring together the theologies of the Testaments, producing an Old Testament theology, a New Testament theology, and eventually a true biblical theology. Today such an achievement is theoretical rather than actual, for no one has yet produced this work. However, Ladd's *Theology of the New Testament* is a good first step.[28] Now we await the next stage.

The most beneficial type of biblical theology for the church is a thematic study. Whenever a local church is trying to respond to a controversial issue like divorce, women in leadership roles, or even music in the church, the final arbiter must always be Scripture. However, all too often the Bible is handled poorly, with proof texts (verses that are taken out of context and, without exegetical study, used to "prove" a point) being presented to settle the issue. There are many problems with proof texting. First, the verses are seldom studied in their contexts. But without context there actually is no meaning. Any passage can be manipulated to mean anything. This is how David Koresh "proved" to his naive followers that he was God's chosen "evil Messiah."[29] He took passages from Revelation and a few other books and twisted them to mean what he said.[30] Second, only the God-intended meaning should be used, but proof texting never bothers with detailed analysis of passages to find out what God was saying through the inspired authors. One could prove virtually any view by stringing together passages without concern for their intended meaning. A famous example combines the statement "Judas went away and hanged himself" with "Go thou and do likewise" as biblical support for suicide. Third, proof texting places one's own desires ahead of God's. It follows the dictum "the end justifies the means." In order to accomplish the desired goal, one ignores God's truth and manipulates the Bible to make certain that it teaches what one wants.

When a situation in a church demands theological input, thematic study is the best approach. It utilizes the so-called synthetic (or cross-section) method: themes are traced through the various books and historical periods of the Bible. The strength of this method is its assumption of the unity of Scripture. While the synthetic method recognizes the great diversity of the parts and traces each theme through various traditions, the primary purpose is to study the interconnections that tie together the individual perspectives of the writers.

When we do such a study, we will keep in view the "progress of revelation." That is, we will be studying not just the issue, but the historical process by which God revealed the relevant truths to Israel and the early church. As we trace themes historically through the biblical period, it becomes obvious that God sometimes revealed a divine truth slowly, no doubt because it took a great deal of time for fallible human beings to assimilate it. Some truths were, of course, communicated relatively quickly. God revealed his covenant name, Yahweh, to Moses at the burning bush (Exod. 3:16). Other truths were relatively slow in coming. Resurrection and the afterlife did not appear with any clarity until Daniel 12:1–3, 13, and the doctrine developed throughout the intertestamental period, climaxing of course in the New Testament. In the Old Testament, monogamy was the general rule, but polygamy was allowed in the upper classes (Abraham, David, Solomon) well into the New Testament period. Monogamy was not mandated until Jesus and Paul. We must try to remain aware of this progress of revelation in the biblical period.

Recognition of progressive revelation will keep us from a common error that occurs when dogma is drawn from the Old Testament. Most of us are aware of the teaching that Jesus has fulfilled the law (Matt. 5:17–20), which in one sense has become obsolete (Heb. 8:13). However, we do not always realize this when determining laws for the church today. Many people argue that certain regulations continue to be binding on us and prove it by quoting Old Testament passages. For instance, some fundamentalist groups argue that it is wrong to wear shorts. Quoting the regulation that a priest wear "linen undergarments . . . reaching from the waist to the thigh" (Exod. 28:42–43) and "next to his body" (Lev. 6:10; 16:4), they claim that shorts are to be worn only as underclothes and not in public. Others preach the necessity of "storehouse tithing" on the basis of Malachi 3:10 ("Bring the whole tithe into the storehouse"). In both cases the demands are not repeated in the New Testament, and it is doubtful whether Christians today are under any such requirements. The key is to note how God developed his revelation on such issues. Those mentioned only in the Old Testament were meant for Israel and not for the church. Tithing, for instance, is not a New Testament mandate. However, the New Testament expands the Old Testament teaching by stressing sacrificial and cheerful giving, which means for us that giving should *begin* at 10 percent.

To sum up, biblical theology for most of us consists of gathering together all the passages that address an issue or doctrine. At the start we see how each writer treats the issue. Then we note the movement of the teaching from one writer or tradition to another; we follow the historical progress of revelation to see how God developed the understanding of his people through the biblical period. Finally, we put our study of the material together to ascertain the theology of Israel and the early church on the issue. For many of us, this sounds like an impossible task that will take several lifetimes. However, there are certain shortcuts that will help greatly. We can collect the material through inductive Bible study, reading through each biblical book in turn and noting those passages that speak to the issue. In a church, particular books can be assigned to individual members, and a team can collect the material. Another shortcut is to center on those books that emphasize the issue or contain more material than do the others.

In studying discipleship I would center on Matthew, Mark, Luke-Acts, and Paul. In Matthew we discover that the Great Commission (28:18–20) demands not just that we evangelize, but that we "make disciples of all nations." This concludes Matthew's central teaching on discipleship as an entry-level requirement for all who would follow Jesus. The type of half-hearted follower found in many of our churches is not even allowed in the Gospels!

Mark stresses discipleship from the start, beginning three main sections with, respectively, the call of the disciples (1:16–20; note that Jesus is the active agent—"I will make you fishers of men"), their commissioning (3:13–19; note the threefold purpose of discipleship—to "be with him," to preach, to have authority over demons), and their mission (6:7–13; note the emphasis on dependence on God rather than their own abilities). Yet after that positive beginning Mark emphasizes the problem of failure—hardness of heart (6:52; 8:17), spiritual blindness (8:18), misunderstanding (8:31–33), and even desertion (14:27, 50–52). The answer is to surrender to Jesus, who will meet us in our "Galilee" (14:28; 16:7).

In Luke-Acts the radical demands of discipleship come to fullest expression. To be a disciple we must surrender all and follow Jesus totally. Luke especially emphasizes giving up earthly possessions. In the Magnificat, Mary celebrates God's choice of the humble and the poor over the proud and the rich (1:51–53). John the Baptist tells his followers to give their extra possessions to the needy (3:11). Jesus at the start of his ministry defines his work as preaching to the poor and infirm (4:18–19) and in the Beatitudes contrasts the poor and the rich (6:20–26). Discipleship means that everything is to be surrendered, even family and a "place to lay [one's] head" (9:57–62). God must be in control of all possessions (12:13–21), and the disciple must live for heavenly rather than earthly treasure (12:22–34). Above all, the follower must count the cost and be ready to surrender all (14:25–33). In Acts we see these principles carried out as the early church "had everything in common" and lived not to accumulate possessions but to help one another (2:42–47; 4:32–35). In the Gospels and Acts it is clear that discipleship is a complete surrender of all earthly ties in order to follow Jesus with the whole heart.

In Paul discipleship centers on two concepts: being an "imitator" and an "example" for others. Both terms appear in Philippians 3:17 and 1 Thessalonians 1:6–7. To "imitate" means both to pattern one's life after and to obey the one we seek to emulate. In Paul it is clear that the pattern is "imitate me as I imitate Christ." Our task is to follow Christ, and as we do so, to lead others with us in this, life's ultimate pilgrimage. Thus we become an "example," a blueprint for others to pattern their lives after. Another aspect of Pauline discipleship is the pronoun "one another." There are approximately forty uses of this term in Paul, most of them focusing on one of the various aspects of discipleship as members of the church learn to live for "one another."[31]

As we can see, biblical theology is very fruitful for the task of theological formulation. It is not an elitist discipline open only to the professional who can spend hours and hours at a desk. It is something any of us who are willing to do deep Bible study can take part in. It is something that the church desperately needs in its search for truth. Many current debates that have the potential to split the church can be resolved if we will learn to do basic biblical theology in our search for answers.

3. Historical Theology

The second intermediate step (along with biblical theology) between exegesis and systematic theology is historical theology. All of us are part of a confessional community and as such partake of church history. Our community's tradition plays a formative role in our process of interpretation, informing us in terms of our understanding of texts and guiding the stages by which we organize our thoughts into a system. Historical theology traces the background of our community theology and studies the development of our traditions. As Stuart Hall says, "Historical theology is the study of theology from the point of view of the past. It asks what has been said of God and his ways, by whom and when and why it was said. Theology, like most modern intellectual studies, is to a large extent conducted histori-

cally. The truth in the present is set out as an interpretation of
what has been said or written in the past."[32] As such, historical
theology also informs our study of the individual doctrines that
we hold and the issues that we investigate in the theological
process of exegesis to biblical to historical to systematic theology. By emphasizing the historical background to our dogmatic
decisions, historical theology is extremely valuable in the
hermeneutical process. Through it we can both see how a doctrine has evolved through the history of the church and study
the growth and development of our own confessional tradition.

In a sense there is direct continuity between biblical and historical theology. As biblical theology traces the development of
doctrine in the history of Israel and the early church (the progress
of revelation), so historical theology traces the development of
doctrine in the emerging and contemporary church (the progress
of illumination). The first studies the theological thought-
patterns of the biblical period, the second the theological
thought-patterns of the periods of church history. Historical
theology, then, shows how the church performed its own biblical theology at each stage of its development. Thus it stands technically between biblical and systematic theology, noting how later
communities of faith understood the biblical doctrines and organized them into systems. The process of revelation has two
stages—inspiration of the normative data recorded in the Bible
(the focus of biblical theology), and illumination of the interpretation of those data throughout the history of the church (the
focus of historical theology). Through these disciplines the theologian has two controls (biblical and historical theology) for
determining the shape and validity of doctrine for the present
church (the focus of systematic theology).

For instance, in studying the twin doctrines of election and
security, it is important to realize that debates with the heretic
Pelagius led Augustine to form his system. John Calvin, who
refined Augustine's system, was part of the Reformation reac-

tion against the extremes of Roman Catholic theology. Jacobus Arminius, in developing his system, was reacting against extremes in Dutch Calvinism, and John Wesley was reacting in part to Calvinist tendencies in the Anglican church. Of course, this is only a cursory survey, but the point is that systems have a history and can be traced in part to reactions against extreme positions. By noting such social forces in the formation of dogma in church history, we can see ourselves in bold relief and allow the Bible rather than dogmatic debates to control our own doctrinal decisions. Moreover, we can become more truly biblical by seeing how our own preunderstanding is shaped by the debates of the past. Historical theology provides a valuable check upon our own similar tendencies to read biblical ideas in light of our own needs. It makes us aware of the fallacy of reading contemporary issues into ancient texts. At the same time, we see models like Calvin and Wesley who were able to surmount their times and develop a truly biblical system. Whether we agree with their final systems or not, they are the giants whom we are privileged to emulate.

As Hans-Georg Gadamer has noted, a major hermeneutical breakthrough has occurred in our time: community understanding (the developing tradition) provides categories for interpreting texts and theology. Community exegesis has two aspects: dialogue with the past community of faith by means of historical theology, and dialogue with the present community of faith via current commentaries and theological works as well as dialogue both within and between communities and denominations. Both aspects provide a necessary challenge to our preconceived theologies so that we become text-driven and not just idea-driven. Church history makes us aware of the historical place held by our current faith community and helps us to be more open to challenges from other communities. For through church history we more clearly see and distinguish those issues that have been settled for centuries (cardinal doctrines) and those that have been and undoubtedly always will be debated by faith communities with the same commitment to an inerrant, infallible Scripture. This produces in us a humility and openness to truth that allows the biblical text to speak clearly on such issues. For historical theology forces us to see our theological position and our understanding of the biblical teaching in light of the big picture (the historical development of doctrine).

Many readers are undoubtedly asking, "But how can I do such an analysis of the historical background? I have no training and very little time." When we first consider the task of historical theology, it certainly does seem daunting, if not impossible. Studying the Bible is hard enough, but nearly two thousand years of church history in addition? Come on, get real!

Actually, we cannot do an in-depth study of the historical basis of our faith or of particular doctrines. However, with a little reading of the right book on church history, we can increase our knowledge greatly.[33] The next step is to buy a couple of good tools for tracing issues and debates through church history.[34] It is surprising how rapidly knowledge will increase and how much fun it can actually be.

Take the doctrine of election, which we have already noted. Finding a basic discussion of Augustine's or Arminius's wrestling with the issue will not be too difficult; by perusing articles and using indexes, one can often find quite a bit of data in a short time. A church going through a major study of a difficult issue would do well to consult some experts from a seminary acceptable to the leaders. Important decisions deserve, indeed require, consultation. Seminary profs are glad to lend their expertise in the service of the church. A few phone calls and at times meetings between church leaders and authorities on historical theology can point the way to answers to confusing issues.

Finally, I hardly mean that no theological study can be complete without historical theology. The average person can of course study issues entirely on the basis of biblical teaching and not have to consult historical theology. Rather, I am saying that historical theology provides an invaluable control in developing a complete systematic theology.

4. Systematic Theology

Systematic theology is rightly called the queen of the biblical sciences. It summarizes every aspect of the study of Scripture. As I have said elsewhere:

> One begins with the traditional views inherited from the chosen theological community (such as Methodist, Reformed or evangelical, liberal). This is the preunderstanding with which one begins. Then the theologian traces a particular issue (such as atonement or eschatology) through Scripture inductively, determining which passages speak to the issue. At this stage exegetical study searches for the exact nuances in each passage that addresses the doctrine and begins to organize the passages in order to determine which aspect of the doctrine each passage teaches. Biblical theology collates the results and determines the belief of Israel and the early church on the issue. Next the theologian traces the issue through church history to see how it was developed to meet different needs in different eras. This tells how the doctrine was contextualized in the past and provides invaluable positive as well as negative clues for the recontextualization of the doctrine for our own time.[35]

It is the task of systematic theology to oversee all these aspects. It is not merely a specialized field responsible only for philosophical contextualization, that is, for reworking the results of biblical theology via the lessons of historical theology and thereby giving the already developed data a new and contemporary organization. Rather, the professional theologian is a Renaissance genius responsible to rework every aspect in the service of the belief structures of the church today.

Yet again the layperson does not have to be overwhelmed by the sheer amount of data to be collected and sifted. Most of this work has already been done by scholars, so the task at hand is to do an inductive study of the biblical material, then to compare and evaluate the data supplied by those who have traveled the road before. For instance, when studying eschatology, particularly debates regarding the rapture or the millennium, we will collect the relevant passages (Matt. 24:29–31; 1 Cor. 15:51–57; 1 Thess. 4:13–17; 2 Thess. 2:1–12; Rev. 3:10 for the rapture; primarily Rev. 20:1–10 for the millennium), then exegete with commentaries, collate the material to discover the unifying theme, and compare the conclusions of theologians on the various sides to see which option best fits the data.

There are two types of systematic theology. We can seek a field theory or systemic model that unites all of dogma into a single logical, organized system (such as the Reformed, Arminian, dispensational, Anabaptist, or charismatic theologies), or we can study an individual theological issue in light of the larger set of doctrines of which it is a part. Unlike the more comprehensive types of biblical theology, however, the first is not something that should be relegated to professionals. We all owe it to ourselves and to the Lord to work out our theology and understand how it all fits together. We need to decide whether we are Reformed or dispensational or Anabaptist, whether Calvinist or Arminian, whether charismatic or noncharismatic. We need to realize how our eschatology informs and builds upon our doctrine of God, how our view of the Holy Spirit impacts our approach to spiritual gifts, how our position on women in the church is part of our ecclesiology (doctrine of the church). This is not an impossible task, as long as the church is doing its part. We are not meant to study these things in splendid isolation, as if we were monks in a cloister. Our home church should be teaching us these things, and theological awareness should be one of the goals of Bible-study groups. We need to study not only Isaiah and Matthew and Romans, but the doctrine of the Trinity, the sacraments (baptism and the Eucharist), and the twin doctrines of sin and salvation. We must study our theological heritage and learn respect for the other Christian faith communities with whom God wants us to relate and work in evangelizing the world.[36]

In developing a model for our belief system, it is critical to work out how the aspects of that system relate to one another. Each detail is a minimodel and part of the larger dogmatic model that characterizes the system. Let me use as an example the systems we have mentioned several times in this chapter, Calvinism and Arminianism (see figure 4). Each part (total depravity, election, regeneration, security, etc.) is a model in itself summarizing the community's understanding of many biblical passages and many decisions of historical theology down through the centuries. The purpose of the overarching models is to view each of the systems as a whole and to allow us to compare them. Through the models we can structure the theological details and view their relationships to each other. This knowledge is an indispensable aid in the search for doctrinal truth, for it enables us to make sense of the whole as well as the parts. A high view of biblical authority demands a search for a systematic theology that reflects our understanding of the unity of Scripture and its teachings as well as provides a basic statement of our community's faith system. We are seeking a theoretical model that best conceptualizes and restates the eternal truths of the Word of God as our church understands them. Each model in figure 4 organizes the biblical doctrine of soteriology on the basis of the tradition, community understanding, and experience of its respective group.

We also must understand that each model is highly debated within its respective community. I have attempted to provide generic models that fit the larger communities as a whole. In fact, however, most of the details are highly debated even within

Figure 4
The Calvinist and Arminian Models of Soteriology

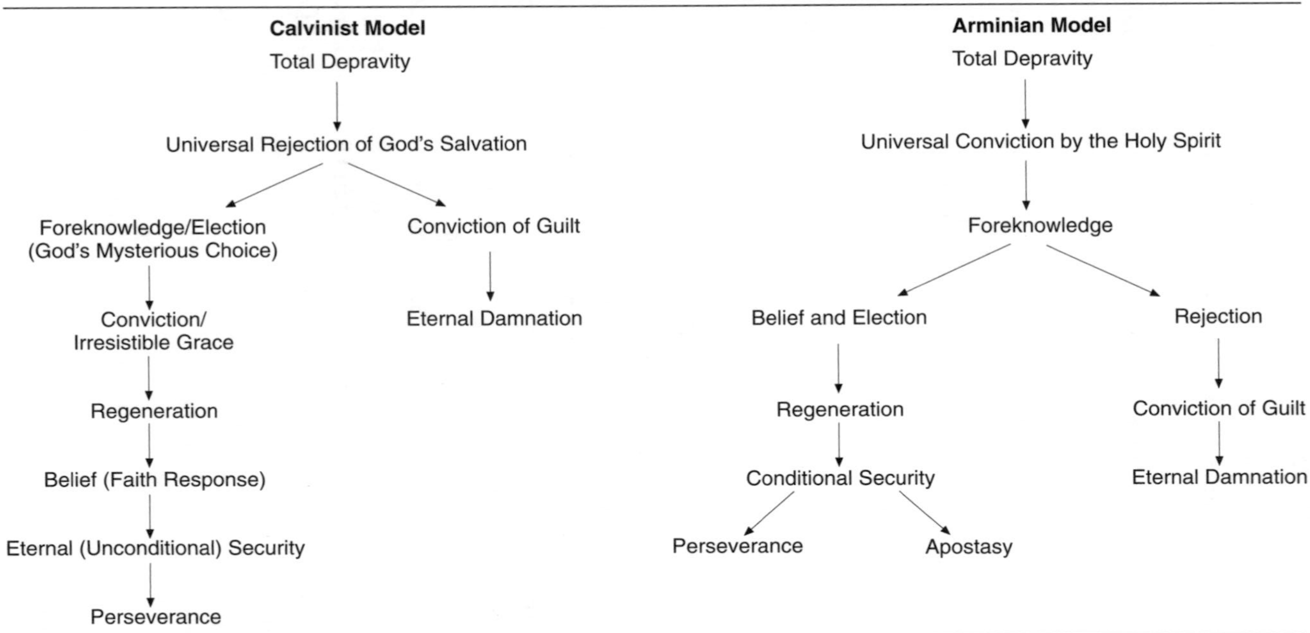

Arminian Model

Total Depravity → Universal Conviction by the Holy Spirit → Foreknowledge

Foreknowledge → Rejection → Conviction of Guilt → Eternal Damnation

Foreknowledge → Belief and Election → Regeneration → Conditional Security → Apostasy / Perseverance

Calvinist Model

Total Depravity → Universal Rejection of God's Salvation

Universal Rejection of God's Salvation → Conviction of Guilt → Eternal Damnation

Universal Rejection of God's Salvation → Foreknowledge/Election (God's Mysterious Choice) → Conviction/Irresistible Grace → Regeneration → Belief (Faith Response) → Eternal (Unconditional) Security → Perseverance the Calvinist and Arminian camps. For instance, Calvinists differ in their views regarding the relationship of regeneration to belief, and within the doctrine of election there is a huge debate as to whether election is single (God has chosen those who are to be his children) or double (both those going to heaven and those going to damnation are predestined to their fate). Within the Arminian camp there is debate as to whether election is primarily corporate (the church is elect, but individuals enter on the basis of their free decision) or individual (each one foreknown by God is elect); the extent of conditional security is also debated (that is, under what conditions can apostasy occur?). Each community must work out its own model of its doctrinal system. Also, note that the models represented here relate only to soteriology (the doctrine of salvation). This issue also has to be placed within the larger system of theology and related to doctrines of the Trinity, the church, eschatology (last things), and so on.

Finally, it is very helpful for each group to understand the doctrinal models of the other communities of faith. These models are heuristic, that is, they are continually open to clarification, improvement, and change. Much of the antagonism between our denominations and church groups has resulted from a failure to understand each other and especially to understand that all the groups are wrestling with the very same issues. The models summarize particular views of the whole of Scripture. We give our own model strong assent, but it is not inerrant. Each is open to modification or even replacement if the biblical data so indicate. Placing competing models side by side helps in two ways: we understand our own better by seeing it in bold relief beside the other, and we gain a greater appreciation for the other model. No model has permanent status, though the Calvinist and Arminian have stood the test of time. We affirm one or the other (or more likely a modification of one of them), but we need to hold our views with humility. All of us are comfortable with our own views, but we need to respect the perspective of others. Both are based on Scripture, and both are serving (and used by!) God.

Still, most of us will spend more time thinking about individual doctrines than about our whole system of faith. How do we develop our views on the millennium, for instance? First, we acquaint ourselves with the issues, that is, the pre-, post-, and amillennial positions. Second, we collect all the biblical passages that might discuss the subject. For the sake of comprehensiveness, we should do this both inductively by reading through the Bible and deductively by noting those passages that are mentioned by books and dictionary articles on the general topic. For instance, we will note Old Testament passages on the future blessed state of Israel (e.g., Isa. 11–12; 40:9–11; 52:7–12; Jer. 33:17–22; Amos 9:14–15), and such New Testament passages as Matthew 25:31–46; 1 Corinthians 15:22–28; 1 Thessalonians 4:13–18; and the primary text of Revelation 20:1–10. Then we will do as much exegetical study of these passages as we can, collating them and asking to what extent they speak of a future earthly reign of Christ after his return (premillennialism), an earthly millennial reign before his return (postmillennialism), or a present symbolic rather than future earthly reign (amillennialism). After that we will trace the issue in church history to see how the debate has developed and to study possible models for the doctrine.[37] Finally, we will put all this together and either decide that one of the options is the best expression of the biblical data or refine the existing theological models as necessary.

For both types of systematic theology (working with whole systems or individual doctrines) one more item is absolutely critical. Harold O. J. Brown makes a very strong case that theology, to be done properly, must be based on faith. "Theology *as an intellectual discipline, as a science,* must begin with faith." He defines theology as a "reflective self-understanding of faith" and points

out that while unbelievers can achieve an intellectual understanding of theology, they are not open to the "scientific" or real
world within the discipline.[38] At the other end of the spectrum
(from pretheology to posttheology), once theology is understood, it cannot be relegated only to the sphere of knowledge,
but must be lived out in obedience.[39]

The Bible is very clear that theology is not merely to be understood, but to be believed and obeyed. The New Testament does
not enjoin mere apprehension, for "knowledge" is commitment, an act of the will. For instance, consider the New Testament passages on eschatology, the return of Christ. In every single passage stressing the parousia (second coming), the major
emphasis is not upon the fact of his return, but upon the
believer's ethical responsibility in light of his return. In the
Olivet Discourse (Mark 13; Matt. 24–25), Jesus centers not
just upon judgment but upon spiritual vigilance ("be alert" in
Mark; the parables in Matthew). First Corinthians 15 concludes
with "Stand firm. Let nothing move you"; 1 Thessalonians
4:13–5:11 concludes with "Encourage one another and build
one another up"; 2 Thessalonians 2:1–15 concludes with "Stand
firm and keep a strong grip on the truth" (LB). Every New Testament eschatological passage leads into ethics, and this is true
of nearly every doctrine. We must live our faith, not merely
affirm it!

How do we verify or validate our theological decisions? We
begin by recognizing that those decisions have no automatic
authority. Since all doctrinal assertions are theological constructs
or finite approximations that represent biblical truth, they have
a certain tentativeness about them. Their accuracy is a moot
point, often highly debated in the larger theological community.
Furthermore, there is a historical dimension, as we interact with
the tradition behind our position as well as with competing traditions that challenge our position. David Tracy notes four stages
in theological formulation:

1. We approach the text (Scripture or another theological classic) with a certain preunderstanding.
2. We react to the claims of the text with faith and recognition.
3. We begin a critical dialogue not only with the text, but with its history, effects, and interpretations.
4. We utilize hermeneutical principles to retrieve and reinterpret traditions and then make our conclusions public.[40]

From this it is clear that there is no simple straightforward path from the Bible to theological assertions, nor are our decisions automatic reproductions of biblical teaching. Rather, we filter all the material derived from Scripture through a complex mesh of preunderstanding, tradition, and philosophical perspective. Thus each doctrine must be assessed and validated on the basis of scriptural and historical viability. It is even good to give our choices a percentage value in terms of our confidence that the model fits the evidence. For instance, I feel almost 100 percent certain that my view on the deity of Christ is correct, but only 80–90 percent sure regarding my middle position on the charismatic issue (i.e., the gift of tongues still occurs today, but, being controlled by the Spirit, is not for everyone) or my view regarding the second coming (premillennial posttribulationism). I feel very much at home regarding these views, but the biblical data lead me to be more certain about some issues than about others.

Therefore the process of verification is a complex one, especially since the church worldwide will continue to debate many of these doctrines until the Lord returns. We all know some individuals who will even be arguing with the Lord that he has not considered all the data! It is best not to be quite so sure of oneself on theological issues that are not absolutely clear in Scripture. A hermeneutics of humility is by far the best approach. Nevertheless, to the best of our ability we need to make theological decisions and validate them. The best method for verifying a model or theological position is critical realism (see p. 82). This method, while assuming that a premise is a valid representation of the way things are, refuses to presume that it is an *exact* model; rather, it is an *approximate* model that must be tested. This testing occurs via a reexamination of the evidence, the interpretations, and the extent to which the model fits the evidence. We ask first whether the model fits the biblical data (criterion of coherence), whether it summarizes all the evidence (criterion of comprehensiveness), whether it is a better depiction than competing models (criterion of adequacy), whether it is a logical and viable model (criterion of consistency), whether it will be accepted for a long time to come (criterion of durability), and whether it is acceptable to more than one faith community or is acceptable within only one tradition (criterion of cross-fertilization). These criteria of course do not prove a doctrine; however, they help serious Christians to discern the viability of various theological options and to test their own conclusions.[41]

After we have developed our theological position and tested it, one final issue remains. Are we ready for the consequences? There is a political aspect to theological decisions, for certain changes in a position could cost a person a job (for a minister or teacher) or role in church. Even more importantly, they could split the church, as in the sad but true story regarding the gifted young pastor at the opening of this chapter. In every tradition there is a demand for adherence to the key beliefs of the movement. Often these are critical doctrines, and the demands are completely valid. There must be controls against dangerous speculations and false teaching. In fact, both in the New Testament and in the early church, theology developed largely in reaction to just such heresies. Other times, however, the issues were not critical, and the church split should have been avoided. The Gospel of John balances unity (10:16; 17:20–23) with purity (10:8–10, 12–13; 15:6). The church must be united, which means openness toward positions that are not clearly false, and discipline against positions that are (see also Matt. 18:7–20). We must maintain a firm stance against heresy but learn to agree to disagree on issues that are not cardinal doctrines.

But how do we know? Heresy hunting has become almost a fad in the last few years, but sadly in many cases there should not have been any such charges. There is a great difference between serious error and disagreement over a doctrine on which the Scripture itself is not completely clear. Whenever I begin a new ministry, I tell the congregation that we have two options as to how we handle a controversial view (see figure 5). We can exercise intolerance or tolerance toward the view and those who teach it. We must realize that each option entails a corresponding action. If we believe that we should be intolerant, we must discipline the persons involved, asking them either not to teach or to leave the church or, in severe cases, excommunicating them as false teachers. If we believe the situation calls for tolerance, we will dialogue on the issue and agree to disagree. But how do we know when to do one or the other? It depends on the issue. If it is a cardinal doctrine (namely a doctrine that is essential to Christianity and absolutely mandated in Scripture for all believers), we must be intolerant. If it is a noncardinal doctrine (namely

Figure 5
A Perspective on Theological Debates

Issue	Attitude	Action
Cardinal Doctrine ———————▶	Intolerance ———————▶	Discipline
	Middle Position: Denominational Distinctives	
Noncardinal, Nonessential Doctrine ———————▶	Tolerance ———————▶	Dialogue
	Criterion: The Word of God Control: The History of Dogma	

a doctrine that is not absolutely clear in Scripture and not essential to the faith), we should be tolerant.

But how do we know whether an individual issue is a cardinal doctrine? The criterion for orthodoxy of course is the Word of God. But the Word of God doesn't work in this case (I say it this way to get your attention). Everyone with a hobbyhorse issue thinks that the Scripture proves it is a cardinal doctrine. So we need a control, and that control is the history of dogma. Church history tells us which issues have never been decided except within individual traditions. From church history we also know what are the cardinal doctrines. They have been decided by the church as a whole for centuries—the Trinity, the deity of Christ, the indissoluble union of Jesus' humanity and his deity, substitutionary atonement, salvation by grace alone, the return of Christ. Other issues are open questions and have never been settled (at this point I always use an example that I know is not divisive in the church—usually the rapture or the doctrine of election). Church history tells us that groups with a high view of Scripture have never come to agreement on these issues and probably never will before the Lord returns. Whenever a controversial issue comes up, we should look at it through the grid of church history and decide whether or not we are going to let it be divisive. If the heresy hunters would only use such criteria, they would understand what constitutes heresy and attack far fewer people!

One further point: In a middle position between cardinal and noncardinal doctrines are "denominational distinctives." These are doctrines that, while not cardinal dogma, have become mandated within particular denominations. In most Reformed denominations, Calvinism (election, eternal security, sometimes limited atonement) is mandated; in other denominations, a particular view on charismatic gifts or the rapture is required. In my denomination (the Evangelical Free Church) the millennial issue is crucial; all pastors and the faculty at my seminary have to be premillennial. While these are not cardinal doctrines, they are mandated by the denomination. But even though we require a specific position, we still try to teach our people tolerance so that they will not look down on or refuse to work with groups of a different persuasion.

My view is that on all these issues God has allowed his revealed Word to remain less than completely clear so that we will keep the opposing ideas in tension and be balanced. God does not prefer Arminians over Calvinists or vice versa. Nor does he prefer amillennialists over premillennialists or egalitarians over advocates of male leadership. Rather, God has deliberately allowed more than one perspective in his Word so that we can find the middle position and be balanced. An equally important point is that this does not mean we should not try to determine which system is more biblical. One cannot be both a Calvinist and an Arminian. A person cannot be unconditionally secure and yet be able to lose salvation. While God allows both positions and indeed wants us to be balanced between divine sovereignty and free will, between security and responsibility, one of them is theologically wrong. We owe it to the Word of God to work out our position and to give it our allegiance. However, we should at the same time hold our position on such issues with humility and learn respect for those of other persuasions.

A Sample Theology

It is critical to put all this in perspective. I am not setting an impossible task requiring an IQ of 200 and an unlimited amount of time. I believe any layperson or church can do theology with enjoyment and great benefit. To answer the question of this chapter, "Yes, we can get theology from the Bible." Theology is developed at many levels, and it is critical to find one's own level. At the basic level, we all make theological decisions whenever we attend a Bible study, listen to a sermon, or think about our Christian walk. At a deeper level, we can work through doctrinal issues for ourselves or think about the theological implications of what we will teach or preach. A Sunday school teacher theologizes at one level, a pastor preaching a series at another level. The Christian leader preparing an ordination paper summarizing one's personal theology must work carefully through the issues. At the deepest level would be those writing major theological treatises or systematic theologies. It is their responsibility to work very carefully and completely at every aspect of the task discussed in this chapter. Yet even here there are levels. A person producing a single-volume theology over a period of a couple of years will obviously not have the time to do deep work on individual issues. A magnum opus, a multivolume work taking years, sometimes decades, will probe as deeply and extensively into the subject as possible. Few of us will ever attempt such a work, but we can all do theology at the first three levels, and we can all search Scripture to work out our system as a whole or to refine our views on individual doctrines.

Let me use the debate over the charismatic movement, particularly over tongues (or glossolalia), as a model. It was in my first pastorate that I began to study this issue in earnest. A close relative said that I must speak in tongues to be "baptized in the Spirit" and to be a mature Christian. A close friend said that in his opinion the tongues in evidence today are not from God because the gift ceased with the events covered in the New Testament. This was confusing, so I decided to find out for myself which view was better. I began by studying the Bible and getting a couple of books on the issue. The first goal was to gather together all the passages that speak to the issue. After a few days of reading, I had discovered Numbers 11:26–30; 1 Samuel 10:5–13; 19:18–24; Isaiah 28:11; Joel 2:28–30; Mark 1:8 and parallels; 16:15–20 (though several versions consider this passage an addition to Mark); Acts 2:1–13; 4:31; 8:14–19; 9:17; 10:44–48; 19:1–7; 1 Corinthians 12–14; and Hebrews 2:3b–4.

Next I began to study the passages. Some of the Old Testament passages (Num. 11; 1 Sam. 10, 19) concern ecstatic prophecies that prophets spoke under divine power, but there is no real evidence these were a form of tongues. Joel 2 is quoted by Peter in Acts 2:16–21. This makes tongues a fulfilment of prophecy, but Joel does not mention glossolalia directly, just visions, dreams, and prophesying. The "baptism with the Holy Spirit and with fire" that John the Baptist mentions in Mark 1:8 and Matthew 3:11 probably refers to both Pentecost and divine judgment (perhaps the final judgment), but does not really prophesy the later gift of tongues.

Next I researched Acts, with its repetitions of the Pentecost outpouring of the Spirit and of tongues. I was struck by two things. First, some of the recipients of the gift (the Samaritans [ch. 8] and the Gentiles [ch. 10]) were outsiders to the church, and the Jerusalem Christians were leery of accepting them; the Baptist's disciples (ch. 19) somehow did not know that the Spirit had come. Second, there is no hint in Acts that everyone who was converted experienced the gift of tongues; only special groups received it. It suddenly struck me that the Pentecost repetitions in Acts 8 and 10 were not intended as a paradigm for every new believer, but as a divine message to the Jewish Christians that God had chosen a new ethnic group to be part of the church, and that they had to be accepted. The purpose of the event in Acts 19 was to tell the Baptist's disciples to follow Jesus not the Baptist. In other words, Acts cannot be used to mandate tongues for every Christian.

Working through 1 Corinthians 12–14 took a fair amount of time, but the richness of this passage made the effort worth it. As I considered the passage carefully, I began to realize that the problem was not glossolalia per se, but the Corinthians' misuse of it. They made tongues the greatest of the gifts and so established a false hierarchy. Paul corrected this by placing tongues further down the list (12:28). Tongues are not just "spiritual gifts" *(pneumatika),* but even more are "grace gifts" *(charismata).* They do not center on the individual, but on the God who gives them. For tongues to be viable, they must be interpreted (12:10; 14:5, 13–19).

As I pondered 1 Corinthians, several points became clear. First, Paul is not antitongues; he spoke in tongues (14:18) and wished that everyone could speak in tongues (14:5). Second, not everyone can speak in tongues; he asks, "All do not speak with tongues, do they?" (12:30 NASB), expecting the readers to answer, "No." Third, it is the Holy Spirit, not we, who controls the gift, and he works with all the gifts, not just one, giving "them to each one, just as he determines" (12:11). Fourth, there is no basis here for arguing that the charismatic gifts have ceased. Some try to see this in 13:10, "when perfection comes, the imperfect disappears." They believe that "perfection" cannot refer to Jesus, since the Greek term is neuter ("perfect thing"); so they interpret it as the close of the canon: the imperfect will cease when the "perfect revelation" will have been received. However, it probably refers to the "perfect age." This is made likely by verse 12, which speaks of the time when "we shall see face to face."

Hebrews 2:3b–4 has also been used to argue that tongues would cease. It says that God used signs and wonders to testify to his salvation as preached by the apostles. Some scholars take this to mean that once the Apostolic Age had passed, supernatural testimony would no longer be needed, so the miraculous gifts would cease. However, as I looked at this in context, I realized that apostolic proclamation is not stressed. Hebrews 2:3b–4 says only that testimony to God's salvation is *a* purpose, not *the only* purpose of tongues. So the passage does not really teach that tongues and other gifts have ceased.

When I collated all the data, I realized they supported neither the position expressed by my relative nor that expressed by my friend. Rather, the evidence seemed to favor a middle position, that God can still use tongues, interpretation, healing, and prophecy, but the Spirit determines who receives them. In other words, we are not to worry about *what* gifts we are to receive; instead, we are to be ready to receive and use the ones the Spirit has for us. A. B. Simpson, founder of the Christian and Missionary Alliance, said it best with his "Seek not, forbid not."[42] C. M. Robeck discusses Paul's guidelines for exercising the gift of tongues.[43] Since tongues come from God, they must manifest the qualities of the God of peace and bring unity and understanding to the church. Paul's use of the metaphor of the body in 1 Corinthians 12:12–31 makes it clear that tongues are to build up the body and contribute to the corporate fellowship of the church. When members exercise the gift, they must do so "in a fitting and orderly way" (14:26–40) and must edify the assembly (14:12). If the gift disrupts or brings dissension, it must be controlled for the greater good. The gift must never become an end in itself, but must always be utilized for personal worship and the growth of the whole community. When misused, it becomes a "sign of judgment" against the unbeliever in the congregation, who thinks it a manifestation of madness (14:23). So it must be used carefully and at all times be kept under strict control, first the control of the Spirit and second of the church.

Then I felt I had to trace the issue through church history to check whether my conclusions fit how God had guided Christian activity and what the giants of the church's past had taught. Before Augustine, there was little evidence of any opposition to tongues. Irenaeus, Tertullian, and Origen were all supportive of the gift. It wasn't until the Montanist movement and the reactions of Augustine and Chrysostom that opposition developed. There was little evidence of glossolalia in the Middle Ages except among missionaries who, late in that era, claimed the gift in terms of speaking in the languages of the people they evangelized (e.g., Vincent Ferrer, Francis Xavier). Both Martin Luther and John Calvin, however, felt that the gift was viable. In his

1 Corinthians commentary Calvin wrote against those who rejected tongues, saying that Paul went so far as to commend them. John Wesley in his journal said that the greater danger was not overemphasis but suppression or denial of spiritual gifts. While there were some outbreaks of glossolalia (it did occur among the Jansenists, Quakers, Irvingites, and Shakers), they were few and far between. Nevertheless, there is too little evidence to support the view that the gift ceased, and no evidence to support the view that all believers are to experience it. The twentieth-century growth of the Pentecostal movement, however, must be recognized, and there is again no evidence to think that God has not allowed the movement and used it. The more I looked at the historical data, the more I believed that the Pentecostal and non-Pentecostal segments of the church had to cease their animosity and begin to work together.[44]

Finally, I tried to put all the data together and place them into my larger system of theology. Glossolalia and the other gifts are difficult to categorize, since the doctrine of spiritual gifts bridges from pneumatology (doctrine of the Holy Spirit) to ecclesiology (doctrine of the church). In my opinion, it is time for the next theological genius to give us a new way of organizing theology. The old Aristotelian method of rigid categories (doctrine of Scripture, doctrine of God, doctrine of Jesus Christ, etc., concluding with the doctrine of last things) does not work very well, because the doctrines overlap and inform one another. Therefore, I decided to keep the issue of spiritual gifts right where I had placed it, between the Holy Spirit and the church. The Holy Spirit controls tongues and the other charismatic gifts and disburses them on the basis of the divine will. The church receives the benefit of these gifts in terms of greater spiritual fervor, edification, and a heightened sense of the divine presence. Through my study I became convinced that my task is to wait upon the Lord and seek to use the gifts he has given me for the benefit of his people. I must not worry about what gifts I am to have and how gifted I am to be. Nor am I to compare myself with those who have gifts I would like or those who have the same gift but in greater measure than I. Rather, I should rejoice in both groups and thank the Lord for the gifts I have received, considering them to be a sign of divine grace. Finally, I must be humble about my middle position. I believe it is correct, but it is possible that the Pentecostal or the cessationist position is correct instead. I must always be in dialogue with these other positions and let them challenge my conclusions.

To summarize: there are four steps in moving from Scripture to theology—exegesis, biblical theology, historical theology, and systematic theology. Technically, it is best to follow the path of all four in order, as demonstrated above. In actuality, however, it is not absolutely required to do so. We can, of course, simply study the Bible and work out the theology that best fits the passages. However, three cautions are necessary. We must try to be as comprehensive as we can, for it is exceedingly dangerous to build theology on our favorite passages, since the tendency is to ignore those portions of the Word that challenge our position. In a sense, the passages that give us difficulty are more important than our favorites, for they drive us back to a more balanced position. Second, we must study the passages as deeply as we can in accordance with the process laid out in chapter 2, for all of us tend to read our own meaning into biblical texts, especially if theology is at stake. Third, we must develop a theological synthesis that covers *all* the passages, those that favor our pet theories and those that do not. That way, our theology will sum up all the biblical data rather than be based upon a few favored proof-texts.

Recommended Reading

Gerhard Hasel. *Old Testament Theology: Basic Issues in the Current Debate.* 4th ed. Grand Rapids: Eerdmans, 1991. Also, *New Testament Theol-*

ogy: Basic Issues in the Current Debate. Grand Rapids: Eerdmans, 1978. Two of the best volumes discussing the methodology of and issues in doing biblical theology in the two Testaments.

The Lion Handbook: The History of Christianity. Edited by Tim Dowley. 2d ed. Batavia, Ill.: Lion, 1990. An excellent study of the development of dogma in light of church history. It is very readable and a good source for tracing doctrines in their historical development.

Doing Theology in Today's World. Edited by John D. Woodbridge and Thomas E. McComiskey. Grand Rapids: Zondervan, 1991. An excellent discussion of the methodology for doing theological studies. It includes articles on the various schools (e.g., liberal, feminist, Reformed, charismatic).

Notes

Chapter 1: "Can We Trust the Bible?"

1. See John D. Woodbridge, *Biblical Authority: A Critique of the Rogers/McKim Proposal* (Grand Rapids: Zondervan, 1982), for a detailed account of the historical development of this doctrine.

2. We say "original autographs" because what we have today are not the original manuscripts but later copies with many alternate readings. To get back to what Jeremiah or Isaiah or John or Paul originally said, we have to engage in textual criticism. For more on this, see Paul D. Feinberg, "The Meaning of Inerrancy," in *Inerrancy,* ed. Norman Geisler (Grand Rapids: Zondervan, 1980), 296–97.

3. See Jack B. Rogers and Donald K. McKim, *The Authority and Interpretation of the Bible: An Historical Approach* (San Francisco: Harper and Row, 1979).

4. See Karl Barth, *Church Dogmatics,* 13 vols. (Edinburgh: T. and T. Clark, 1936–69), vol. 1, part 1, pp. 124–28.

5. J. I. Packer, "Encountering Present-Day Views of Scripture," in *The Foundation of Biblical Authority*, ed. James Montgomery Boice (Grand Rapids: Zondervan, 1978), 71.

6. See Barth, *Church Dogmatics*, vol. 1, part 2, pp. 507–30.

7. Roger Nicole, "The Neo-Orthodox Reduction," in *Challenges to Inerrancy: A Theological Response*, ed. Gordon R. Lewis and Bruce Demarest (Chicago: Moody, 1984), 138–44.

8. See Rudolf Bultmann, "The New Testament and Mythology," in *Kerygma and Myth*, ed. Hans Werner Bartsch, rev. ed. (New York: Harper and Row, 1961), 1–44, where he rejects the Bible's "three-storied universe" of God, humans, and the demonic forces. According to Bultmann, the world is controlled by natural not supernatural forces.

9. See Paul Tillich, *Systematic Theology,* 3 vols. (Chicago: University of Chicago Press, 1951–63), 1:107–30.

10. See the excellent article by Fred H. Klooster, "Revelation and Scripture in Existentialist Theology," in *Challenges to Inerrancy*, ed. Lewis and Demarest, 175–214.

11. Karl-Otto Apel, Jürgen Habermas et al., *Hermeneutik und Ideologiekritik* (Frankfurt: Suhrkamp, 1971), 41–44, 133–50, as discussed in Grant R. Osborne, "Meaning in a Meaningless World: Hermeneutics and the Scholar," *A Journal for Christian Studies* 12 (Fall 1993): 7–8.

12. Rosemary Radford Ruether, "Feminist Interpretation: A Method of Correlation," in *Feminist Interpretation of the Bible*, ed. Letty M. Russell (Philadelphia: Westminster, 1985), 113.

13. For the quotations see Packer, "Encountering Present-Day Views," 75, 81n.

14. Geoffrey W. Bromiley, "Hans Küng," in *Evangelical Dictionary of Theology*, ed. Walter A. Elwell (Grand Rapids: Baker, 1984), 616.

15. Edgar V. McKnight, *Postmodern Use of the Bible: The Emergence of Reader-Oriented Criticism* (Nashville: Abingdon, 1988), 13.

16. See Jacques Derrida, *Of Grammatology*, trans. G. C. Spivak (Baltimore: Johns Hopkins University Press, 1976).

17. See Stanley Fish, *Is There a Text in This Class? The Authority of Interpretive Communities* (Cambridge, Mass.: Harvard University Press, 1980). On Fish and Derrida see Grant R. Osborne, *The Hermeneutical Spiral: A Comprehensive Introduction to Biblical Interpretation* (Downers Grove, Ill.: InterVarsity, 1991), 380–85.

18. John MacArthur, Jr., *Is the Bible Reliable?* (Panorama City, Calif.: Word of Grace Communications, 1988), 5.

19. For an excellent study on this topic see Wayne Grudem, "Scripture's Self-Attestation and the Problem of Formulating a Doctrine of Scripture," in *Scripture and Truth*, ed. D. A. Carson and John D. Woodbridge (Grand Rapids: Zondervan, 1983), 19–27.

20. Gleason Archer, "The Witness of the Bible to Its Own Inerrancy," in *Foundation of Biblical Authority*, ed. Boice, 89.

21. Grudem, "Scripture's Self-Attestation," 28–35.

22. Ibid., 42–43.

23. Most helpful here is the excellent discussion by Craig Blomberg, "The Jesus Tradition in Acts-Revelation," in *The Historical Reliability of the Gospels* (Downers Grove, Ill.: InterVarsity, 1987), 219–33.

24. See Ralph P. Martin, "Creed," and Grant R. Osborne, "Hermeneutics/Interpreting Paul," in *Dictionary of Paul and His Letters*, ed. Gerald F. Hawthorne, Ralph P. Martin, and Daniel G. Reid (Downers Grove, Ill.: InterVarsity, 1993), 190–92, 392–93.

25. Grudem, "Scripture's Self-Attestation," 46.

26. For an excellent dramatic presentation of the data in this section in the format of a formal debate, see Murray J. Harris, *3 Crucial Questions about Jesus* (Grand Rapids: Baker, 1994), 31–64.

27. Clarence Walhout, "Texts and Actions," in Roger Lundin, Anthony C. Thiselton, and Clarence Walhout, *The Responsibility of Hermeneutics* (Grand Rapids: Eerdmans, 1986), 69, 72–76.

28. See William Lane Craig, *The Son Rises: The Historical Evidence for the Resurrection of Jesus* (Chicago: Moody, 1981), 23–24.

29. Craig, *Son Rises,* 27–28, observes that a person holding this view "must believe (1) that twelve poor fishermen were able to change the world through a plot laid so deep that no one has ever been able to discern where the cheat lay, (2) that these men gave up the pursuit of happiness and ventured into poverty, torments, and persecutions for nothing, (3) that depressed and fearful men would have suddenly grown so brave as to break into the tomb and steal the body, and (4) that these imposters would furnish the world with the greatest system of morality that ever was."

30. See Grant R. Osborne, *The Resurrection Narratives: A Redactional Study* (Grand Rapids: Baker, 1984), 276.

31. See Craig L. Blomberg, "The Legitimacy and Limits of Harmonization," in *Hermeneutics, Authority, and Canon*, ed. D. A. Carson and John D. Woodbridge (Grand Rapids: Zondervan, 1986), 139–74.

32. The following is drawn from Osborne, *Resurrection Narratives*, 281–92; Murray J. Harris, *From Grave to Glory: Resurrection in the New Testament* (Grand Rapids: Zondervan, 1990), 157–63; George E. Ladd, *I Believe in the Resurrection of Jesus* (Grand Rapids: Eerdmans, 1975), 91–93; and John Wenham, *The Easter Enigma: Are the Resurrection Accounts in Conflict?* (Grand Rapids: Zondervan, 1984).

33. See Blomberg, *Historical Reliability*, 117–27; and Grant R. Osborne, "Redaction Criticism," in *Dictionary of Jesus and the Gospels,* ed. Joel B. Green, Scot McKnight, and I. Howard Marshall (Downers Grove, Ill.: InterVarsity, 1992), 662–68.

34. See Ben F. Meyer, *The Aims of Jesus* (London: SCM, 1979).

35. In actuality Luther was saying that James, with its lower Christology and its soteriology, is not as deep as Paul's writings.

36. David G. Dunbar, "The Biblical Canon," in *Hermeneutics, Authority, and Canon*, ed. Carson and Woodbridge, 358–60.

37. Ibid., 301–3; Andrew E. Hill and John H. Walton, *A Survey of the Old Testament* (Grand Rapids: Zondervan, 1991), 18–22; and D. A. Carson, Douglas J. Moo, and Leon Morris, *An Introduction to the New Testament* (Grand Rapids: Zondervan, 1992), 488–89.

38. The Apocrypha refers to a group of intertestamental books that includes 1 and 2 Esdras, Tobit, Judith, Additions to Daniel (Prayer of Azariah, Song of the Three Young Men, Susanna, Bel and the Dragon), Additions to Esther, the Prayer of Manasseh, the Epistle of Jeremiah, Baruch, Ecclesiasticus (Sirach), the Wisdom of Solomon, 1 and 2 Maccabees. Some Septuagint manuscripts add 3 and 4 Maccabees and the Psalms of Solomon.

39. Dunbar, "Biblical Canon," 308–12; and James H. Charlesworth, "Apocrypha," in *Anchor Bible Dictionary*, ed. David Noel Freedman, 6 vols. (New York: Doubleday, 1992), 1:292–94.

40. Dunbar, "Biblical Canon," 356.

41. Walter Liefeld, *New Testament Exposition: From Text to Sermon* (Grand Rapids: Zondervan, 1984), 143.

42. Josh McDowell, *Evidence That Demands a Verdict: Historical Evidences for the Christian Faith* (San Bernardino, Calif.: Campus Crusade for Christ, 1972), 48.

43. William S. LaSor, David A. Hubbard, and Frederic W. Bush, *Old Testament Survey: The Message, Form, and Background of the Old Testament* (Grand Rapids: Eerdmans, 1982), 102–7.

44. Dewey M. Beegle, *Scripture, Tradition, and Infallibility* (Grand Rapids: Eerdmans, 1973), 308.

45. F. F. Bruce, *The New Testament Documents: Are They Reliable?* 5th ed. (Grand Rapids: Eerdmans, 1960), 60.

46. Rudolf Bultmann, *Jesus Christ and Mythology* (New York: Scribner, 1958), 15.

47. Phillip E. Johnson, "Shouting 'Heresy' in the Temple of Darwin," *Christianity Today* 38.12 (Oct. 24, 1994): 22, 24.

48. Ibid., 25. See also his *Darwin on Trial* (Downers Grove, Ill.: InterVarsity, 1992).

49. Winfried Corduan, *Reasonable Faith: Basic Christian Apologetics* (Nashville: Broadman, 1993), 157–58. For further excellent discus-

sion, see also Colin Brown, *Miracles and the Critical Mind* (Grand Rapids: Eerdmans, 1984).

50. William Lane Craig, *Reasonable Faith: Christian Truth and Apologetics,* rev. ed. (Wheaton, Ill.: Crossway, 1994), 142–44.

51. Richard Swinburne, *The Concept of Miracle* (London: Macmillan, 1970), 26.

52. Note the cover article of *Time* magazine for April 10, 1995, "Can We Still Believe in Miracles?" (pp. 64–73). It is clear that those who reject miracles, even in this secular society, are in the minority.

53. Arthur Holmes, *Faith Seeks Understanding* (Grand Rapids: Eerdmans, 1971), 25–29.

54. Ibid., 29–32.

55. I. T. Ramsey et al., *The Miracles and the Resurrection* (London: S.P.C.K., 1964), 1–30.

56. C. S. Lewis, *Miracles,* in *The Best of C. S. Lewis* (New York: Iverson Associates, 1969), 243–60.

57. Walter C. Kaiser, *Hard Sayings of the Old Testament* (Downers Grove, Ill.: InterVarsity, 1988), 108. See also J. A. Thompson, *Deuteronomy: An Introduction and Commentary* (Downers Grove, Ill.: InterVarsity, 1974), 73, 128–29.

58. Walter C. Kaiser, *More Hard Sayings of the Old Testament* (Downers Grove, Ill.: InterVarsity, 1992), 123–26.

59. Kaiser, *Hard Sayings,* 123.

60. Gordon D. Fee and Douglas Stuart, *How to Read the Bible for All It's Worth: A Guide to Understanding the Bible* (Grand Rapids: Zondervan, 1981), 183.

61. Kaiser, *Hard Sayings,* 125.

62. See I. Howard Marshall, *The Gospel of Luke: A Commentary on the Greek Text* (Grand Rapids: Eerdmans, 1978), 325–26; Grant R. Osborne, "The Evangelical and Redaction Criticism: Critique and Methodology," *Journal of the Evangelical Theological Society* 22.4 (1979): 314; and D. A. Carson, "Matthew," in *The Expositor's Bible Commentary,* ed. Frank E. Gaebelein, vol. 8 (Grand Rapids: Zondervan, 1984), 245, 247.

63. Joachim Jeremias, *The Eucharistic Words of Jesus* (New York: Scribner, 1966).

64. Anne Jaubert, *The Date of the Last Supper* (Staten Island, N.Y.: Alba, 1965).

65. See William L. Lane, *The Gospel according to Mark,* New International Commentary on the New Testament (Grand Rapids: Eerdmans, 1974), 496–98.

66. Douglas J. Moo, "The Law of Christ as the Fulfillment of the Law of Moses," in *The Law, the Gospel, and the Modern Christian,* ed. Wayne G. Strickland (Grand Rapids: Zondervan, 1993), 351.

67. E. P. Sanders, *Paul and Palestinian Judaism* (Philadelphia: Fortress, 1977).

68. See Douglas J. Moo, *Romans 1–8* (Chicago: Moody, 1991), 212–18; and Stephen Westerholm, *Israel's Law and the Church's Faith: Paul and His Recent Interpreters* (Grand Rapids: Eerdmans, 1988).

69. Moo, "Law of Christ," 359.

Chapter 2: "Can We Understand the Bible?"

1. William W. Klein, Craig L. Blomberg, and Robert L. Hubbard, Jr., *Introduction to Biblical Interpretation* (Dallas: Word, 1993), 4.

2. See Fred H. Klooster, "The Role of the Holy Spirit in the Hermeneutical Process: The Relationship of the Spirit's Illumination to Biblical Interpretation," in *Hermeneutics, Inerrancy, and the Bible*, ed. Earl D. Radmacher and Robert D. Preus (Grand Rapids: Zondervan, 1984), 451–72.

3. John Calvin, *Institutes of the Christian Religion,* 1.9.3.

4. On critical realism see Paul Hiebert, "The Missiological Implications of an Epistemological Shift," *TSF Bulletin* 8.5 (1985): 12–18; and Grant R. Osborne, *The Hermeneutical Spiral: A Comprehensive Introduction to Biblical Interpretation* (Downers Grove, Ill.: InterVarsity, 1991), 310–11.

5. E.g., Robert A. Traina, *Methodical Bible Study* (New York: Ganis and Harris, 1952); Irving L. Jensen, *Independent Bible Study* (Chicago: Moody, 1963).

6. A different outline may fit the grammar of the passage better. Given that vv. 16–17 are a statement made by outsiders ("on that day they will say," v. 16a), the first point might be the command (v. 14), the second point the reason (v. 15), and the third point a concluding summary (vv. 16–17, which expand the ideas in v. 15cd in reverse order [v. 16 = v. 15d, no need to fear; and v. 17 = v. 15c, God's presence with his people]).

7. For recent discussion supporting this view, see J. D. G. Dunn, "Prayer," in *Dictionary of Jesus and the Gospels*, ed. Joel B. Green, Scot

McKnight, and I. Howard Marshall (Downers Grove, Ill.: InterVarsity, 1992), 618–19.

8. See Klein, Blomberg, and Hubbard, *Biblical Interpretation*, 160–61.

9. For a basic presentation see Osborne, *Hermeneutical Spiral,* 41–63. More-detailed information can be found in the better grammars. For Greek see F. Blass and A. Debrunner, *A Greek Grammar of the New Testament and Other Early Christian Literature*, trans. and rev. by Robert W. Funk (Chicago: University of Chicago Press, 1961); and Nigel Turner, *Syntax*, vol. 3 of *A Grammar of New Testament Greek*, ed. James H. Moulton et al., 4 vols. (Edinburgh: T. and T. Clark, 1963). For Hebrew see Ronald J. Williams, *Hebrew Syntax: An Outline,* 2d ed. (Toronto: University of Toronto Press, 1976); and Bruce K. Waltke and M. O'Connor, *An Introduction to Biblical Hebrew Syntax* (Winona Lake, Ind.: Eisenbrauns, 1990).

10. For a useful discussion of possible errors to avoid in studying grammar, including the verb, see D. A. Carson, *Exegetical Fallacies* (Grand Rapids: Baker, 1984), 67–90.

11. Walter C. Kaiser and Moisés Silva, *An Introduction to Biblical Hermeneutics: The Search for Meaning* (Grand Rapids: Zondervan, 1994), 55–56.

12. James Barr, *The Semantics of Biblical Language* (Oxford: Oxford University Press, 1961), 218. Though daunting, this is a phrase I always use in lay Bible-study seminars. Once it is understood, no other phrase so succinctly states the problem.

13. Barr, *Semantics*, 218, writing against K. L. Schmidt, *"ekklēsia,"* in *Theological Dictionary of the New Testament,* ed. Gerhard Kittel and Gerhard Friedrich, trans. Geoffrey W. Bromiley, 10 vols. (Grand Rapids: Eerdmans, 1964–76), 3:501–36.

14. Kaiser and Silva, *Biblical Hermeneutics*, 34–44.

15. Anthony C. Thiselton, *New Horizons in Hermeneutics* (Grand Rapids: Zondervan, 1992), 16–19, 597–601. Reflecting the research of J. L. Austin and the speech-act theory of John Searle, these three elements are called, respectively, the locutionary, illocutionary, and perlocutionary functions.

16. For Hebrew that means the classic lexicon of Francis Brown, S. R. Driver, and Charles A. Briggs, eds., *A Hebrew and English Lexicon of the Old Testament* (Oxford: Clarendon, 1962); and the *Lexicon in Veteris Testamenti Libros,* ed. Ludwig Koehler and Walter Baumgartner, 2 vols. (Grand Rapids: Eerdmans, 1958). For Greek the standard is

A Greek-English Lexicon of the New Testament and Other Early Christian Literature, ed. W. Bauer, W. F. Arndt, F. W. Gingrich, and F. W. Danker (Chicago: University of Chicago Press, 1979).

17. *Theological Dictionary of the New Testament*, ed. Kittel and Friedrich; *New International Dictionary of New Testament Theology,* ed. Colin Brown, 4 vols. (Grand Rapids: Zondervan, 1975–78); and *Exegetical Dictionary of the New Testament,* ed. Horst Balz and Gerhard Schneider, 3 vols. (Grand Rapids: Eerdmans, 1990–93).

18. See Osborne, *Hermeneutical Spiral*, 90–92.

19. Gordon D. Fee, *New Testament Exegesis: A Handbook for Students and Pastors* (Philadelphia: Westminster, 1983), 84–85.

20. Edwin Yamauchi, *The Stones and the Scriptures* (New York: Lippincott, 1972), 146–58.

21. Colin J. Hemer, *The Letters to the Seven Churches of Asia in Their Local Setting* (Sheffield: JSOT, 1986), 186–91.

22. See Osborne, *Hermeneutical Spiral*, 129–31.

23. Barry J. Beitzel, *The Moody Atlas of Bible Lands* (Chicago: Moody, 1985), 102–3. All the cities conquered by Joshua lay in the highlands, for Israel could not challenge the Canaanite war chariots in the plains.

24. See André Lemaire, "Education (Israel)," in *Anchor Bible Dictionary,* ed. David Noel Freedman, 6 vols. (New York: Doubleday, 1992), 2:306–7.

25. For background in general see J. A. Thompson, *Handbook of Life in Bible Times* (Downers Grove, Ill.: InterVarsity, 1986); on the Old Testament see Roland de Vaux, *Ancient Israel: Its Life and Institutions* (New York: McGraw-Hill, 1961); and A. S. Van der Woude, *The World of the Old Testament* (Grand Rapids: Eerdmans, 1989); on the New Testament see Everett Ferguson, *Backgrounds of Early Christianity* (Grand Rapids: Eerdmans, 1987); and Joachim Jeremias, *Jerusalem in the Time of Jesus: An Investigation into Economic and Social Conditions during the New Testament Period* (Philadelphia: Fortress, 1969); a more popular work, somewhat dated but still helpful, is Henry Daniel-Rops, *Daily Life in the Time of Jesus* (New York: Hawthorn, 1962). InterVarsity Press is developing a very helpful set explaining the biblical background passage by passage; the New Testament volume has already been published—Craig S. Keener, *The IVP Bible Background Commentary: New Testament* (Downers Grove, Ill.: InterVarsity, 1993).

26. Norman Gottwald, *The Tribes of Yahweh: A Sociology of the Religion of Liberated Israel* (Maryknoll, N.Y.: Orbis, 1979).

27. J. Duncan M. Derrett, "The Parable of the Unjust Steward," in *Law in the New Testament* (London: Darton, Longman, and Todd, 1970), 48–77.

28. J. A. Fitzmyer, "The Story of the Dishonest Manager (Lk 16:1–13)," *Theological Studies* 25 (1964): 23–42.

29. Gordon D. Fee and Douglas Stuart, *How to Read the Bible for All It's Worth: A Guide to Understanding the Bible* (Grand Rapids: Zondervan, 1981), 61–65.

30. This could lead to a revision of the outline. On grammatical grounds (vv. 8b–9 constitute a single sentence) we previously began the second main point with v. 8b. However, we now see that conceptually vv. 7–8 can be a unit, since the nouns in v. 7 are repeated as verbs in v. 8b. This would make our points vv. 7–8, v. 9, v. 10, and v. 11.

Chapter 3: "Can We Get Theology from the Bible?"

1. David F. Wells, *No Place for Truth, or, Whatever Happened to Evangelical Theology?* (Grand Rapids: Eerdmans, 1993), 5.

2. Richard A. Muller, *The Study of Theology: From Biblical Interpretation to Contemporary Formulation* (Grand Rapids: Zondervan, 1991), vii.

3. Charles R. Swindoll, *Growing Deep in the Christian Life* (Portland: Multnomah, 1986), 13.

4. Ibid., 12.

5. David Coffin, letter to the editor, *Christian Century* 111.22 (July 27–Aug. 3, 1994): 733; cf. John B. Cobb, Jr., "Faith Seeks Understanding," *Christian Century* 111.20 (June 29–July 6, 1994): 642–44.

6. Os Guinness and John Seel, eds., *No God but God: Breaking with the Idols of Our Age* (Chicago: Moody, 1992), 11.

7. Wells, *No Place for Truth,* 78.

8. Ibid., 76, 86, 130–32.

9. Ibid., 80.

10. Guinness and Seel, eds., *No God but God,* 151–74 (adapted from Os Guinness, *Sounding Out the Idols of Church Growth* [Fairfax, Va.: Hourglass, 1992]).

11. Guinness and Seel, eds., *No God but God,* 155.

12. Ibid., 157.

13. Wells, *No Place for Truth,* 101.

14. Ibid., 113–14.

15. Ibid., 207–11.

16. Ibid., 233–34.

17. Richard Mouw, "Ending the Cold War between Theologians and Laypeople," *Christianity Today* 38.8 (July 18, 1994): 27.

18. Wentzel Van Huyssteen, *Theology and the Justification of Faith: Constructing Theories in Systematic Theology*, trans. H. F. Snijders (Grand Rapids: Eerdmans, 1989), 128.

19. For a good discussion of tradition in the Catholic sense, see Avery Dulles, *The Craft of Theology: From Symbol to System* (New York: Crossroad, 1992), 87–104. Vatican II confirmed the teaching of the Council of Trent that Scripture and tradition together constitute the Word of God.

20. Gordon Kaufman, "Doing Theology from a Liberal Christian Point of View," in *Doing Theology in Today's World*, ed. John D. Woodbridge and Thomas E. McComiskey (Grand Rapids: Zondervan, 1992), 397–415.

21. Paul J. Achtemeier, *The Inspiration of Scripture: Problems and Proposals* (Philadelphia: Westminster, 1980), 118–34.

22. On the referential function of metaphors, see Grant R. Osborne, *The Hermeneutical Spiral: A Comprehensive Introduction to Biblical Interpretation* (Downers Grove, Ill.: InterVarsity, 1991), 299–303; and Janet Martin Soskice, *Metaphor and Religious Language* (Oxford: Oxford University Press, 1985).

23. Richard Gaffin, "Systematic Theology and Biblical Theology," in *The New Testament Student and Theology*, ed. John H. Skilton (Nutley, N.J.: Presbyterian and Reformed, 1976), 44–45.

24. Charles H. H. Scobie, "The Challenge of Biblical Theology," *Tyndale Bulletin* 42.1 (1991): 30–61 (esp. 37–40, 49–50); idem, "New Directions in Biblical Theology," *Themelios* 17 (1991–92): 5–6.

25. Krister Stendahl, "Biblical Theology," in *Interpreter's Dictionary of the Bible,* ed. George A. Buttrick, 4 vols. (Nashville: Abingdon, 1962), 1:419.

26. Elmer A. Martens, "Tackling Old Testament Theology," *Journal of the Evangelical Theological Society* 20 (1977): 123–32 (esp. 123–24).

27. M. M. Thompson, "John, Gospel of," in *Dictionary of Jesus and the Gospels*, ed. Joel B. Green, Scot McKnight, and I. Howard Marshall (Downers Grove, Ill.: InterVarsity, 1992), 376–83.

28. George E. Ladd, *A Theology of the New Testament* (Grand Rapids: Eerdmans, 1974). See also Leon Morris, *New Testament Theology* (Grand Rapids: Zondervan, 1986), shorter but better on the Gospels. Don-

ald Guthrie's *New Testament Theology* (Downers Grove, Ill.: InterVarsity, 1981) follows the "top-down" approach.

29. Koresh's followers were naive in that they were easily duped by arguments that had no connection whatever with what the biblical texts were saying. One of the great problems in the church today is the absence of hermeneutical understanding. Part of the reason why people are drawn in when the Bible is twisted is that they have heard it twisted for years in their Sunday school classes and pulpits. We must develop Berean Christians who "search . . . the Scriptures daily to find out whether these things [are] so" (Acts 17:11 NKJV).

30. See James W. Sire, *Scripture Twisting: Twenty Ways the Cults Misread the Bible* (Downers Grove, Ill.: InterVarsity, 1980). This is an invaluable book, for nearly every error covered occurs in the average church and not just in the cults.

31. See Gene Getz, *Sharpening the Focus of the Church* (Chicago: Moody, 1974), 114–16.

32. Stuart G. Hall, "Theological History and Historical Theology," in *The Threshold of Theology*, ed. Paul Avis (London: Marshall Pickering, 1988), 106.

33. Let me recommend two readable general works on church history: *The Lion Handbook: The History of Christianity,* ed. Tim Dowley, 2d ed. (Batavia, Ill.: Lion, 1990); and Robert G. Clouse, Richard V. Pierard, and Edwin M. Yamauchi, *Two Kingdoms: The Church and Culture through the Ages* (Chicago: Moody, 1993).

34. Two readable works on the history of doctrine are Louis Berkhof, *History of Christian Doctrines* (Grand Rapids: Baker, 1975 reprint); and Sinclair B. Ferguson, David F. Wright, and J. I. Packer, *New Dictionary of Theology* (Downers Grove, Ill.: InterVarsity, 1988).

35. Osborne, *Hermeneutical Spiral*, 286.

36. We also need to understand why we should work with these other denominations and organizations in a larger unity. That is, we should study the connected issues of unity and purity (see pp. 169–70).

37. For good articles see J. W. Montgomery, "Millennium," in *International Standard Bible Encyclopedia*, ed. Geoffrey W. Bromiley et al., 4 vols. (Grand Rapids: Eerdmans, 1979–88), 3:356–61; and Robert G. Clouse, "Millennium, Views of the," in *Evangelical Dictionary of Theology*, ed. Walter A. Elwell (Grand Rapids: Baker, 1984), 714–18.

38. Harold O. J. Brown, "On Method and Means in Theology," in *Doing Theology in Today's World*, ed. Woodbridge and McComiskey, 147–69 (the quotes appear on 148–49 and 150).

39. For a good discussion of the relationship between theology and practice, see Muller, *Study of Theology*, 156–60.

40. David Tracy, *The Analogical Imagination: Christian Theology and the Culture of Pluralism* (New York: Crossroad, 1981), 130–32.

41. See Osborne, *Hermeneutical Spiral*, 307–11, for more on these issues.

42. Quoted in the *Alliance Witness,* 1 May 1963, p. 19.

43. C. M. Robeck, "Tongues," in *Dictionary of Paul and His Letters,* ed. Gerald F. Hawthorne, Ralph P. Martin, and Daniel G. Reid (Downers Grove, Ill.: InterVarsity, 1993), 941–43.

44. See Clark H. Pinnock and Grant R. Osborne, "A Truce Proposal for the Tongues Controversy," *Christianity Today* 16.1 (Oct. 8, 1971): 6–10.